PYTHON FOR DATA ANALYTICS

*A Beginners Guide for Learning
Python Data Analytics from A-Z*

Table of Contents

Introduction

What is Data Analytics?

Data analytics is the analysis of any data (Structured, non-structured) with the help of predictive modeling, mathematical algorithms, statistics and machine-learning techniques to come up with meaningful insight, patterns, behavior and knowledge, which in turn helps in making fact based decisions in business accurately.

Data analytics basically deals with a large volume of data sets, which we call Big Data, to find hidden patterns, market trends, correlations, customer interests and preferences and other useful information in the domains of science, social science and business.

Why is it Needed?

Why did data analytics came into play? Why has it become a necessity for a business to sustain and be ahead of others in competition in the market? Actually, everyone has data. We all talk about the data we record in our systems, but the difference is how we put data into action. The difference comes in organizing, accessing and analyzing our data to attain our objectives in improving performance.

We cannot always rely on guesses and intuition to make critical decisions to run a big business. This is the reason why there is a need to make decisions on facts, logics patterns and behavior. This is where data analytics come into the picture. Data Analytics can answer the below questions:

- What happened?
- How or why did it happen?
- What's happening now?
- What is likely to happen next?

It has a direct influence on the decisions a business makes and on its outcome.

What is the Process of Data Analytics?

Data Analytics is an iterative process with different stages of processing data. Various steps involved in data analysis life cycle are:

1. **Defining and identifying the problem**: It helps in defining the scope, need, market condition and the objective related to the business question. On the basis of the problem, one of the modeling techniques is selected or identified; whichever suits best.

2. **Data Preparation**: Depending on the problem identified and the modeling technique selected, we use some specified methods to acquire, access, clean and prepare data. There can be different types of data from different sources like data from transactional systems, unstructured text files and data warehouses.

3. **Data Exploration**: This is the step where we use various interactive visual charts and graphs to explore data and to find out the trends, relationship and behavioral pattern.

4. **Transform and Select:** At this step, the modelers build models by using the process of data mining, software, algorithms or statistics, mathematics, etc.

5. **Analytical Modeling:** Once the models are built, it gets finalized after registering, testing and approving and declared as ready to use for the recorded data.

6. **Deploy models:** Once the model is approved for use in production, it is applied to new data to create some predictions and insights.

7. **Monitor and assess models:** The performance of the model is regularly monitored. If its performance degrades, it has to be updated, modified or changed.

Chapter 1

Introduction to Python

Python is a powerful modern computer programming language and it is easy to learn. The syntax is simple and it allows the programmers to state their ideas in fewer lines of codes.

It is an interpreted language and no compilation is necessary. It is often used as a scripting language and it is available on Windows, Mac OS and UNIX operating systems. The variable and argument declarations are not necessary as it is determined implicitly. One major advantage of using Python is that it is platform independent and you can run it on any operating system without any issues.

Statements in Python

Every statement is isolated with End of Line (Press Enter in the script). A statement can be anything from assigning a value to reading the input or writing the output on the screen.

We need to keep in mind that Python is a case sensitive language. (e.g. ABC is not similar to abc). Therefore, if we declare a variable with capital letters, then it will not identify it a later stage in the code with small case letters.

For example:

x = 1

y = 2

z = 3

Comments in Python

Comments are used to write the meaning or purpose of the statement. Comments can be ignored by the python interpreter during the runtime. They are very handy to give details about the logic performed in your code for other readers. It ensures that other programmers that are reading your code will understand it easily.

\#   is used to comment a single statement

"""   """   is used to comment multiple statements

For example:

count = 0   # initializing count with zero

"""

     i = 1

     j = 2

     k = 3

     """

Command Line Arguments

The script name and additional arguments are passed to the script in the variable "sys.argv" (sys is a module and argv is a list in python). They are very important to perform the system configuration tasks.

Single space ( ) isolates the arguments in the command line.
"print" is used to print statements in the console.

For example:
import sys
print "Argument number zero: ", sys.argv[0]
print "Argument number One: ", sys.argv[1]
print "Argument number Two: ", sys.argv[2]
print "Argument number Three: ", sys.argv[3]

Execute the script in the below mentioned syntax.
python commandline.py Zero One Two Three

Variables

Variables are used to store values inside them. We can directly define any variable in python and there is no declaration required for variables. In other words, python does not allow declaring variables with data types. There are many types of variables, like Boolean, Character, Integer, Float, String, etc.

For example:

b = False	# Boolean type variable
c = 'd'	# character type variable
i = 20	# integer type variable
s = "Hi"	# string type variable
f = 9.99992	# float type variable
int j = 10	# Syntax Error and not allowed in python

Mathematical Functions

We can perform all mathematical functions in Python easily. Let us see the different type of mathematical functions available in Python.

Numbers:

The operators +, -, * and / work just like in most other languages.

```
>>> 3 + 6
9
```

Here the sum of 3 and 9 is asked and the result 9 is returned. It is just like using the Python interpreter as a calculator.

Just like the addition, as shown above, the other operations subtraction, multiplication and division can be performed. The examples are shown below.

```
>>> 9 - 2
7
>>> 4 * 4
16
>>> 4 / 2
2
```

```
>>> 3 % 2
1
```

In Python, it is possible to use ** operator to calculate powers. The operator % returns the remainder of the division.

For example:

```
>>> 3 ** 4
81
>>> 6 ** 3
216
```

Assigning value to a variable:

The equal sign (=) is used to assign a value to a variable. When we do it, the value in the right side is stored in the variable name present in the left side of = operator.

For example:

```
>>> a = 6
>>> b = 8
>>> a + b
14
>>> a - b
-2
>>> a * b
48
```

The above example shows that the values 6 and 8 are assigned to the two variables a and b. As said earlier, the **variable declaration** is not needed in Python.

```
>>> c = 10.5
>>> d = 4
>>> c + d
14.5
```

```
>>> c - d
6.5
>>> c * d
42.0
```

Data Structures

Sequence

Sequence is a very basic term in python that is used to denote the ordered set of values. There are many sequence data types in python: str, unicode, list, tuple, buffer and xrange.

Tuples

A tuple consists of a number of values separated by commas. Tuples are also a sequence data type in Python, like strings and lists. We need to keep in mind that tuples are immutable. It means that they can't be changed.

The tuples consist of the number of values separated by a comma. The tuples are enclosed in parentheses, while the lists are enclosed in brackets.

Now let us see an example:

```
>>> m = (14, 34, 56)
>>> m
(14, 34, 56)
>>> m[0]
14
```

```
>>> m[ 0:2 ]
(14, 34)
```

Tuples also have the properties like indexing and slicing. Tuples can be nested. Elements in a tuple can be grouped with ()

Now let us see an example:
```
i = 1
j = 2
t1 = i, j           # is a tuple consists to elements i and j
t2 = (3, 4, 5)      # is a tuple consists to elements 3,4 and 5
t3 = 0, t1, t2      # is a tuple consists to elements 0, t1 and t2
print t3            # result is (0, (1, 2), (3, 4, 5))
```

Lists

A list consists of a number of heterogeneous values separated by commas enclosed by [and] and started from index 0. Lists can be used to group together other values. Unlike Tuples, Lists are mutable in nature. In other words, they can be changed by removing or reassigning existing values. Also, new elements can be inserted to the existing ones.

Now let us see an example:
```
>>> a = [1, 2, 3, 4, 5]
>>> a
[1, 2, 3, 4, 5]
```
As strings, lists can also be indexed and sliced.

```
>>> a = [1, 2, 3, 4, 5]
>>> a
[1, 2, 3, 4, 5]
>>> a[0]
1
>>> a[4]
5
>>> a[ 0:2 ]
[1, 2]
>>> a[ 3:5 ]
[4, 5]
```

Unlike strings, **lists are mutable** (i.e. the values can be changed)

```
>>> b = [1, 2, 4, 7, 9]
>>> b
[1, 2, 4, 7, 9]
>>> b[2] = 6
>>> b
```

[1, 2, 6, 7, 9] *# Here the index [2] is changed to 6 (the initial value is 4)*

```
>>> b[0] = 9
>>> b
```

[9, 2, 6, 7, 9] *# Here the index [0] is changed to 9 (the initial value is 1)*

The values in the list can be separated by using comma (,) between the square bracket. Lists can be nested. List can be used as a Stack or a Queue.

For example:

```
list1 = [ 1, 2, 3, 4]
print len (list1)       # returns 4 - which is the length of the list
list1[2]                # returns 3 - which is third element in the list
                        Starts
list1[-1]               # returns 4 - which is extreme last element in
                        the list
list1[-2]               # returns 3 - which is extreme last but one
                        element
list1[ 0:2 ] = [ 11, 22]    # replacing first two elements 1 and 2 with
                        11 and 22
stackList = [ 1, 2, 3, 4]
stackList.append(5)     # inserting 5 from the last in the stack
print stackList         # result is: [1, 2, 3, 4, 5]
stackList.pop()         #  removing 5 from the stack   Last In First
                        Out
print stackList         # result is: [1, 2, 3, 4]


queueList = [ 1, 2, 3, 4]
queueList.append(5)     # inserting 5 from the last in the queue
print queueList         # result is: [1, 2, 3, 4, 5]
del(queueList[0] )      #  removing 1 from the queue   First In First
                        Out
print queueList         # result is: [2, 3, 4, 5]
```

Sets

A set doesn't have any duplicate elements present in it and it is an unordered collection type. It means it will have all distinct elements in it with no repetition.

Now let us seen an example:

```
fruits = ['apple', 'orange', 'apple', 'pear', 'orange', 'banana']
basket = set (fruits)          # removed the duplicate element
                               apple
print 'orange' in basket       # checking orange in basket, result is
                               True
print 'pine apple' in basket   # checking pine apple in basket,
                               result is False
a = set('aioeueoiaeaeiou')     # create a set without duplicates
b = set('bcokcbzo')            # create a set without duplicates
print a                        # a = ['a', 'i', 'e', 'u', 'o']
print b                        #   b = ['z', 'c', 'b', 'k', 'o']
print a & b                    # letters in both a and b  ( A ∩ B )
print a | b                    # letters in either a or b  ( A ∪ B )
print a - b                    # letters in a but not in b ( A – B )
```

Dictionaries

Dictionaries are the data structures in Python that are indexed by keys.

Key and values separated by : and pairs of keys separated by a comma and enclosed by { and }

Lists cannot be used as keys.

Now let us see an example:

```
capitals = { 'AP' : 'Hyderabad', 'MH' : 'Mumbai' }
capitals[ 'TN' ] = 'Chennai'
print capitals[ 'AP' ]    # returns value of AP in the dictionary
del capitals[ 'TN' ]      # deletes TN from the dictionary
capitals[ 'UP' ] = 'Luck now'  # adding UP to the dictionary
print 'AP' in capitals    # checks where AP key exist in dictionary
print 'TN' in capitals
Numbers  = {'1': 'One', '2': 'Two'}
for key, value in Numbers.iteritems() :
    print key, value
```

Strings

In Python, a string is identified by the characters in quotes, such as single ('') and double (""). They can only store character values and are a primitive datatype. Please note that strings are altogether different from integers or numbers. Therefore, if you declare a string "111", then it has no relation with the number 111.

```
>>> print "hello"
hello
>>> print 'good'
good
```

The string index starts from 0 in Python.

```
>>> word = 'hello'
>>> word[0]
'h'
>>> word[2]
'l'
```

Indices may also be negative numbers, to start counting from the right. Please note that **negative indices** start from -1 while **positive indices** start from 0 (since -0 is same as 0).

```
>>> word = 'good'
>>> word[-1]
'd'
>>> word[-2]
'o'
```

The slicing in Python is used to obtain substrings, while index allows us to obtain a single character.

```
>>> word = 'develop'
>>> word[ 0:2 ]
'de'
>>> word[ 2:4 ]
've'
```

Please note that the **starting** position is always included and the **ending** position is always excluded.

D e v e l o p

0 1 2 3 4 5 6 ---- Index value

In the above example, the word is assigned a value develop. Considering the first statement word [0:2], the output is 'de'. Here the starting position 'd' (0th index) is included and the ending position 'v' (2nd index) is excluded. Similarly, in the second statement word [2:4], the starting position 'v' (2nd index) is included and the ending position 'l' (4th index) is excluded.

The important point to be noted in strings that is Python **strings are immutable** (i.e. Strings cannot be changed).

There are many in-built functions available with a String. They are used for various purposes. Let's see some of the basic ones that are most commonly used.

- Len: It is the length function that is used to calculate the number of characters present in the string.

- Lower: It will convert all the uppercase characters present in the string to lowercase letters. Therefore, after using this function, all characters in the string will be small case only.

- Upper: It will convert all the lowercase characters present in the string to uppercase letters. Therefore, after using this function, all characters in the string will be upper case only.

- Split: It helps to split the string in parts by using a delimiter. It can be separated using spaces, new lines, commas, or tabs.

Control Flow Statements

If –else statement

The if-else statement is used to make the choices from 2 or more statements. It becomes helpful when you want to execute a particular statement based on a True or False condition.

The syntax of if statement is:
If condition:
  action-1   # *Indentation*
Else:
  action-2   # *Indentation*

Here the **indentation** is required. The actions action-1 and action-2 may consist of many statements but they must be all indented.

if <expression> :
        <statements>
else :
        <statements>

The example is shown below.
```
>>> e = 6
>>> f = 7
>>> if(e < f):
...    print( 'f is greater than e' )
... else:
...    print(' e is greater than f')
...
```

Output: f is greater than e

```
def  numberProperty1 ( input ) :
    if input % 2 ==  0 :
print input , ' is an Even number '
    else :
print input , ' is an Odd number '
numberProperty1( 10 )   # result is 10 is an Even number
numberProperty1( 11 )   # result is 11 is an Odd number
```

Nested If

It consists of more than 2 statements to choose from.

```
def numberProperty2 ( input ) :
        if input < 0:
                print input , ' is a Negative number '
        elif input == 0:
                print input , ' is Zero '
        else:
                print input , ' is a Positive number '

numberProperty2( -100 )  # -100  is a Negative number
numberProperty2( 0 )     # 0  is Zero
numberProperty2( 100 )   # 100  is a Positive number
```

While Loop

The while loop will execute until the expression is true and it stops once it is false.

The syntax of while loop is:

While expression:

  statement

For example:

>>> a = 1

>>> while(a < 10):

...   print "The number is:" , a

...   a = a + 1

...

The number is: 1

The number is: 2

The number is: 3

The number is: 4

The number is: 5

The number is: 6

The number is: 7

The number is: 8

The number is: 9

The number is: 10

In the above example, the block consists of print and increment statements, it is executed repeatedly until the count is no longer less than 5.

```
def printSeries( start, end, interval ) :
        print " \n "
        temp = start
        while ( temp < end ) :
                print temp,
                temp += interval
printSeries( 1, 11, 1 )   # result is  1 2 3 4 5 6 7 8 9 10
printSeries( 1, 11, 3 )   # result is  1 4 7 10
```

For Statement

Any object with an iteration method can be used in a for a loop in Python. The iteration method means that the data can be presented in list form where there are multiple values in an ordered manner. The syntax of for loop is:

for item in list:
    action   *# Indentation*

The action consists of one or more statements and it must be **indented**. The examples are shown below.

For example:
```
>>> for i in (1, 2, 3, 4, 5, 6, 7, 8, 9, 10):
...     print i
...
1
2
```

3

4

5

6

7

8

9

10

```
>>> list = ['a', 'bb', 'ccc', 'dddd']
>>> for l in list:
...    print l,len(l)
...
a 1
bb 2
ccc 3
dddd 4
```

The above program shows that the values of a list and its length are printed using the for loop.

Functions

A function is a block of organized and reusable code that is used to perform related action. We can break our huge lines of programming code into smaller modules with the help of functions. It also helps in avoiding repetition of code, as we don't need to write the same lines of code again and again. Instead, we can write it once inside a function, and then use the function anywhere in the program.

You need to make sure that the function name is unique.

Rules to define a function in Python
1. In Python, function is defined using the keyword def.
2. The arguments will be placed within the parenthesis ().

Now let us see an example:
>>> def printdetails(name, age):
...   print "Name:", name;
...   print "Age:", age;
...   return;
...
>>> printdetails(name = "Mary", age = 30);
Name: xxx
Age: 30

In the above example 'printdetails 'is the function name and name and age are the parameters.

Syntax of user defined method
def < function name> :
      [< declaration of local variables >]
      [< statements >]

Now let us see an example:

```
Language = "Python"
def printString( input ) :
        print input
def multiply ( x, y ) :
        return x * y
def power( x, y):
        return x ** y
printString( Language )      # returns Python
z = multiply( 10, 20 )
print z          # returns 200 - which is equal to 10 * 20
print power( 10, 2 )   # returns 100 - which is equal to 10 ** 2
```

Accepting inputs during the runtime

raw_input() is a built-in python function provides the facility to accept input during the execution of the script

Now let us see an example:

```
        name = raw_input( "\n Please enter your name : " )
```

This statement provides a message to the user to provide input for name.

Control Statements

Break

The break statement breaks out of the smallest enclosing for or while loop.

Now let us see an example:
```
def primeNumberValidation ( input ) :
    for x in range( 2, input ) :
        if input % x == 0:
            print  input, 'is not a prime number and equals', x, '*',
input/x
            break
        else:
            print  input, 'is a prime number'
primeNumberValidation( 3 )
primeNumberValidation( 14 )
```

Continue

The continue statement continues with the next iteration of the loop.

Now let us see an example:
```
def evenNumbers( start, end ) :
        print "\n\nEven numbers in between ", start , " and ", end
        for n in range( start + 1, end ) :
                if n % 2 !=  0:
```

continue

print n

evenNumbers(1, 11)   # result is 14 is 2 4 6 8 10

evenNumbers(10, 30) # result is 12 14 16 18 20 22 24 26 28

Pass

The pass is a valid statement and can be used when there is a statement required syntactically, but the program requires no action.

Now let us see an example:

while True :

pass   # In condition loop press (Ctrl + c) for the keyboard interrupt

In this example, while followed by pass does not execute any statement.

There is a necessity to include at least one statement in a block (e.g. function, while, for loop etc.)   in these cases, use pass as one statement, which does nothing but includes one statement under ':'

Now let us see an example:

def x() :

pass   # one valid statement that does not do any action

Here pass is considered a statement for the declaration of function x.

String Manipulation

We can use built in functions to manipulate strings in python. The package "string" provides more functions on strings.

For example:

print name = "ABCD XYZ xyz"

print len(name)	# It will return the length of the string name
print list(name)	# It will return the list of characters in name print
name.startswith('A')	# It will return True if name starts with A else returns False
print name.endswith('Z')	# It will return True if name ends with Z else returns False
print name.index('CD')	# It will return the index of CD in name
print 'C'.isalpha( )	# It will return True if C is alpha or returns False
print '1'.isdigit( )	# It will return True if 1 is digit or returns False
print name.lower( )	# It will return a string with lowercase characters in name
print name.upper( )	# It will return a string with uppercase characters in name

Exception Handling

Exceptions are the errors detected during execution and these are not unconditionally fatal.

Exception blocks will be enclosed with try and except statements.

```
try  :
        <statements>
except  <exception type > :
        <statements>
```

Let's see an example:

 # Defining an exception block
```
try  :
        print ( 1 / 0 )
except Exception as excep:
        print "exception : ", excep
```

 # Defining a user-defined exception
```
class UserDefinedException( Exception ) :
        def __init__(self, value):
            self.value = value
        def __str__(self):
            return repr(self.value)
```

 # Raising a user-defined exception explicitly

try:

      raise UserDefinedException(" input is null ")

except UserDefinedException as userdefinedexception:

      print 'userdefinedexception : ', userdefinedexception.value

In the above mentioned program, first (try, except, block) handles Zero division exception.

UserDefinedException is a userdefined exception to raise business exceptions in the program.

Second (try, except) block raises a user defined exception.

Chapter 2

IPython: An Interactive Shell for Python Programming

Introduction

As you begin to learn any new language, you will often find yourself asking, "What should be the ideal environment for my Python development?". To this, my answer is usually, "IPython and a text editor". While a text editor is a basic tool for writing and formatting your programs, you can always replace it with a Python Integrated Development Environment (IDE), such as PyCharm or Spyder, to program in Python. This is because an IDE offers more intelligent code completion and more advanced graphical tools. In addition, some IDEs also offer IPython integration, thereby contributing to the ease of use of Python developers. Regardless, whether you choose to work on a text editor or an IDE, I highly recommend that you make IPython an integral part of your Python programming.

Project IPython started in 2001 as a side project of Fernando Perez with the aim of making a better, more powerful interactive Python shell. Over the past 18 years, it has amassed fame and praise for being a significant tool in the contemporary computing stack of scientific Python. While IPython is not a shell that offers data analytical or computational tools on its own, it is designed to enhance your productivity in interactive programming, as well as software development. Instead of the traditional cycle of programming where you edit, compile and run your code, IPython supports an execute-explore approach. This means that IPython will assist you in your process of exploration and iteration of your data analysis programming. Moreover, it is also closely embedded with an operating system file system and shell.

There's a lot more to IPython than an interactive Python computing environment. For one, it is highly customizable, and for another, IPython also offers a web-based notebook format coupled with a user-friendly GUI console with support for inline plotting and a fast, lightweight parallel computing engine. You'll get to delve further into their details as you follow along with the chapter.

If you're new to IPython, I suggest that you pay close attention to the illustrated examples to get the hang of how things work.

IPython Basics

To launch IPython, just type in the ipython command on your command line:

$ ipython

You can also run random Python expressions and statements by simply typing them in, as you normally would in a text editor, and then pressing Enter. Note than when you type in a variable in IPython, it will return your object in a string format.

Now let us see an example:
In [12]: data = { j : randn() for j in range(9) }
In [13]: data
Out[13]:
{0: 1.3400015224687594,
1: 0.36578355627737346,
2: -1.8315467916607481,
3: 0.24569328634683402,
4: -1.4894682507426382,
5: -1.7920860835730431,
6: 0.5570148722483058,
7: 1.2914683929487693,
8: -0.287602058693052}

Also note that some objects in Python come with an easy reading format at the printing moment that differs from the normal print command. IPython formats (or pretty-prints) Python objects to be more readable. But it could be the case where the standard Python interpreter seems much less readable. You can observe this difference by printing the same dictionary as above in a traditional Python shell.

Now let us see an example:
>>> from numpy.random import randn
>>> values = { j : randn() for j in range(9) }
>>> print values

{0: 1.3400015224687594,   1: 0.36578355627737346,
2: -1.8315467916607481,   3: 0.24569328634683402,
4: -1.4894682507426382,   5: -1.7920860835730431,
6: 0.5570148722483058,   7: 1.2914683929487693,
8: -0.287602058693052}

Tab Completion

A significant improvement IPython has over the traditional Python shell is the *tab completion* feature - a handy feature found in many programming environments for data analysis. While typing expressions in the console, pressing tab after a typed prefix will search the respective namespace for any variables (like functions, objects, etc.) matching your prefix.

Now let us see an example:
In [1]: inter_competitions = 15
In [2]: intra_competitions = 23
In [3]: total_competitions = inter_competitions + intra_competitions
In [4]: in <tab>
in   input   int   inter_competitions   intra_competitions

Here, IPython displayed 2 of the 3 variables I initialized above and also displayed 2 Python keywords in and int and 1 built-in function input because they matched my entered prefix in.

Likewise, you can also use tab completion in IPython to get an object's attributes and methods by typing your object, followed by a period, followed by a tab.

Now let us see an example:

In [5]: population = { 'USA': 327.2, 'Canada': 37.06, 'UK': 66.04 }
In [6]: population.<tab>
population.clear   population.copy   population.fromkeys
          population.get
population.items   population.keys   population.pop
          population.popitem
population.setdefault   population.update   population.values

Similarly, tab completion can be applied to modules:

In [7]: csv.<tab>
csv.Dialect   csv.DictReader   csv.DictWriter   csv.Error
          csv.QUOTE_ALL
csv.QUOTE_MINIMAL   csv.QUOTE_NONE
          csv.QUOTE_NONNUMERIC   csv.Sniffer   csv.StringIO
csv.excel   csv.excel_tab   csv.field_size_limit
          csv.get_dialect

By default, IPython hides attributes and methods beginning with underscores similar to internal attributes and methods so as not to clutter the display and confuse new Python users. In order to view these too, you must proceed with an underscore before pressing tab. To avoid doing this all the time, you can also alter this setting in IPython configuration.

Additionally, tab completion works in a much larger context beyond that of just a single object or a single module. Pressing tab after typing in a file path will display anything on your system's file system that matches whatever you have typed.

Now let us see an example:

In [5]: python_myscripts/ **<Tab>**
python_myscripts/variables_example.py   python_myscripts/ml_test.py
python_myscripts/data_structures.py

In [6]: path = 'python_myscripts/ **<Tab>**
python_myscripts/variables_example.py   python_myscripts/ml_test.py
python_myscripts/data_structures.py

If you are a new IPython user, you will find some methods and attributes hidden, such as underscores so, your display does not get disarranged. In addition, there are other magic and internal "private" methods and attributes that will also be hidden, but by typing an underscore you will be able to unfold them and use the tab-completion tool. The IPython configuration enables this setting so you can see such methods in tab completion and modify the setting any time you want.

Tab completion also facilitates completing a function's argument list. Explore this yourself to find out how!

Introspection

Introspection refers to the general information about an object, such as its type, whether it is a function or instance method - if it is one, string form, length and many other relevant details. As such, preceding or following an object with a question mark will enable you to introspect it.

Now let us see an example:
In [12]: fruits = ['apple', 'orange', 'papaya', 'tangerine']
In [13]: fruits?
Type: list
String Form: ['apple', 'orange', 'papaya', 'tangerine']
Length: 4
Docstring:
list() -> new empty list
list(iterable) -> new list initialized from iterable's items

Let's suppose we wrote the function as follows:
def my_multiplication(a, b):
    """

    Multiply two numbers.
    --Returns--
    the_product : type of arguments
    """

    return a * b

Using a ? on this will yield the docstring as follows:

In [14]: my_multiplication?
Type: function
String Form:<function my_multiplication at 0x5fad359>
File: python_myscripts/<ipython-input-16-3474012eca43>

Definition: my_multiplication(a, b)

Docstring:

Multiply two numbers.

-- Returns --

the_product : type of arguments

Additionally, using a ?? will show the source code of the function too, if possible:

In [15]: my_multiplication??

Type: function

String Form:<function my_multiplication at 0x5fad359>

File: python_myscripts/<ipython-input-16-3474012eca43>

Definition: my_multiplication(a, b)

Source:

def my_multiplication(a, b):
"""

Multiply two numbers.

-- Returns --

the_product : type of arguments
"""

return a * b

Lastly, the ? can also search the entire IPython namespace. If you enclose some characters in a wildcard (*), followed by a ?, it will yield all results matching your expression:

In [16]: np.*nanm*?

np.nanmax

np.nanmean

np.nanmedian

np.nanmin

In this example, IPython returned some functions from the NumPy namespace containing the keyword nanm for mathematical operations that compute the mean, median, maximum and minimum of the data.

Using %run Command

This command enables the execution of any file within your IPython session, same as a Python regular program. Let us assume you have the below script present in ipython_test.py.

For example:

def calculate(a, b, c):

return (a + b + c)

x = 10

y = 15

z = 20

sum = calculate(x, y, z)

Now you can easily run this function by passing the script's name in %run command:

In [17]: %run ipython_test.py

The script will be an empty namespace run, which means no other imports or variables are defined. As a result of this, the < python script.py > command line and the running of the program will be identical. Therefore, all the variables will be set up in the file (globals, imports and functions) and also available in IPython shell as well.

Now let us see an example:
In [18]: z
Out [18]: 20
In [19]: sum
Out [19]: 45

In some cases, the script running in Python demands certain command line arguments. They are located in sys.argv and can be executed on the command line by following the same procedure after the file path.

The usual %run tool will give you access to different variables in the interactive Python namespace regarding to script access, but if you want to define these variables beforehand, use %run -1.

Interrupting Running Code

All Python programs can be stopped immediately, by pressing < Ctrl +C > button simultaneously. This will work with running codes, scripts going through %run or even long-running commands. The final result will be a KeyboardInterrupt.

In some exceptional cases, pressing < Ctrl + C > will not stop the execution of the program. Usually, when you run a Python's piece of code that contains compiled extension modules, you will have two courses of action. Wait for the Python interpreter to get control back or end the Python process via Operating System's task manager.

Executing Code from the Clipboard

This works very fast and enables the code execution in IPython by pasting it directly from the clipboard. It is a great trick to do in practice. For instance, when you are creating a complex Python application, you wish to run a script piece by piece or you want to run and play around that snippet code you've just find on the internet. Instead of pausing at each stage of the script to look the current loaded data and results or simply skipping the creation of a new .py file, you just paste the codes.

By pressing the keys < Ctrl + Shift + V > simultaneously, you can easily paste your current code snippets from the clipboard. However, this mode of pasting equals typing each line into IPython, so line breaks will be treated as a < return >. And if there is a blank line, IPython will read it as the indented block from the code is over. If this continues onto the next line in the block, an IndentationError will be shown. You can see the below example:

```
a = 2
b = 4
if a > 2:
a += 3
b = 6
```

It will not work if you paste it simply like below:

```
In [ 1 ]: a = 2
In [ 2 ]: b = 4
In [ 3 ]: if a > 2:
   ...: a += 3
   ...:
In [ 4 ]: b = 6
IndentationError: unexpected indent
```

Therefore, you should use %paste or %cpaste in order to paste the code into IPython.

Following the error message, we might combine %paste and %cpaste.

%paste will execute any kind of text in the clipboard as a single block in the shell:

```
In [ 5 ]: %paste
a = 2
b = 4
if a > 2:
a += 3
b = 6
## -- End the pasted text --
```

There's a small chance that %paste will not operate on your computer. This is related to your platform and how you installed

Python. But package distributions such as EPDFree, will not present this problem.

%cpaste is analogous, but it also provides you a quick tool for pasting code into:

In [7]: %cpaste
Pasting code; enter '--' alone on the line to stop or use the keys < Ctrl + D >.
:a = 2
:b = 4
:if a > 2:
: a += 3
:
: b = 6
:--

By using %cpaste block, you will be able to paste all the code you wish before running it. This function also gives you the chance to view all the pasted code before the run instance. In case you have accidentally pasted any incorrect code, by pressing < Ctrl + C > you can leave out from the %cpaste prompt.

In next pages, we'll talk about IPython HTML Notebook and its new sharp level to develop block by block analyses, which comes in a browser based format along with executable code cells.

How IPython interacts with various IDEs and editors

Text editors often have third-party extensions that send blocks of code from the editor to a running IPython shell. This is a direct and very common function that the editors like Emacs and vim do. You can visit the IPython website or search in the Internet for more information.

IDEs have integration with the IPython terminal application. Some of them are the PyDev plugin for Eclipse and Python Tools for Visual Studio from Microsoft, among others. This merging process gives you the chance to work both with the IPython console features and the IDE itself.

Keyboard Shortcuts

IPython keyboard shortcuts will be familiar for existing users using the Emacs text editor as well as UNIX bash shell. The shortcuts can be used for navigating the prompt and for interacting with the shell's command history (described in later sections). In the below table, you will find some of the most regular shortcuts used frequently be the programmers.

Shortcut Command	Description
Ctrl + P or Upward Arrow	To search in backward direction in the command history beginning with current position of text
Ctrl + N or Downward Arrow	To search in forward direction in the command history beginning with current position of text
Ctrl + Shift + V	To paste existing text from the clipboard
Ctrl + C	To interrupt the code that is currently running
Ctrl + R	To read the back search history with partial matching
Ctrl + E	Shift the cursor towards end of line
Ctrl + A	Shift the cursor towards start of line
Ctrl + K	Delete text till end of line
Ctrl + F	Shift the cursor forward by 1 character
Ctrl + B	Shift the cursor backward by 1 character
Ctrl + L	To clear the screen

Exceptions and Tracebacks

IPython will show a full stack trace, known as traceback if an exception appears while running any statement or using %run command script. This default tool has the capability to show some context lines at every point of the stack trace.

Let's see an example:

```
In [ 16 ]: %run Chapter2/ipython_error.py
AssertionError                    Traceback (most recent call last)
/home/project/code/ipython/utils/ch2.pyc in execfile(fname, *where)
251              else:
252                  filename = fname
-- > 253             __builtin__.execfile(filename, *where)
home/Chapter2/ipython_error.py in <module>()
25               throws_an_exception()
26
-- > 27          method_called()
AssertionError:
```

Having an additional context is of great importance because the Python's standard interpreter doesn't provide the same. You can easily control the amount of context displayed on the screen using the %xmode command. It will help you to choose from the minimal value to the verbose value.

Magic Commands in IPython

There are some magic commands in IPython that help you control the overall conduct of entire system. You can identify those commands, as they are prefixed with the symbol %. It helps us to check the common tasks like the time taken by a IPython statement for execution.

Now let us see an example:

In [17]: i = np.random.randn(50, 50)

In [18]: %timeit np.dot(i, i)

2500 loops, best of 5: 23.6 us per loop

The IPython system will display the magic commands as command line programs. They will have the additional options that can be shown using ?:

Now let us see an example:

In [5]: x = 2

In [6]: x

Out [6]: 2

In [7]: 'x' in _ip.user_ns

Out [7]: True

In [8]: %reset –f

In [9]: 'x' in _ip.user_ns

Out [9]: False

As long as no variable is defined with the same name as the magic function, it can be used by default without the percent sign. You can enable or disable this automagic feature using %automagic command.

In addition to this, if you type %quickref or %magic, then the special commands that are available will be displayed on the screen.

Here you have a list with the most relevant and critical ones related to save time and improve your computer interaction and development with Python in IPython.

Command	Description
%quickref	To show the quick reference card of IPython
%magic	To show all the available magic commands along with their details
%pdb	To enter debugger automatically after an exception has raised
%reset	To delete all the variable names present in the namespace
%time	To check the execution time of any particular single statement
%paste	To run the code present in the clipboard
%hist	To show the command history

Qt-based Graphical User Interface Console

The framework for Graphical User Interface console consists of a text widget, syntax highlighter, images that are embedded in nature, and additional features of terminal applications. Thus, if PySide or PyQt is already installed in your system, you can directly use it by adding a single line in the command line:

ipython qtconsole --pylab=inline

The Qt console can run multiple processes in tabs and you can easily perform task switching. The console is also compatible with the IPython HTML Notebook application.

Integration with matplotlib and using Pylab Mode

IPython is used worldwide in the area of scientific computing and data analysis because of the fact that its integration is very simple with all the libraries. It's not a problem if you have never used matplotlib before as this will be discussed in detail in later chapters.

When you are creating a matplotlib plot window in a normal Python shell, you will notice that Graphical User Interface event loop will take control of entire running Python session. This will remain until the time you close the plot window. Therefore, it won't suit an interactive & responsive data analysis. To overcome this issue, specific handling has been planned in IPython for every single Graphical User Interface framework. That way it will work with no problems with the shell.

You must add the -- pylab flag (two hyphens) in case you want to run IPython with matplotlib integration.

$ ipython --pylab

This way, a series of things will take place. First, you can create the matplotlib plot windows without any issues, as IPython will be running with the default Graphical User Interface backend integration. After that, an interactive and responsive computing IPython environment will show up at the top level of the namespace.

This setup can be done manually by using %gui, or you can also try with %gui? as well.

Using the Command History

For each command that you execute, IPython keeps a small on-disk database to store text of each of them. This has various uses such as:

- To use minimal typing in order to search, execute, and complete the previous commands that are already executed.

- The history recorded in commands will persist between sessions.

- The input and output history of a file could be logged.

How to Search and Reuse Command History

Possibility of searching and executing previous command is widely considered as a useful tool. As normally happens in code development, you will find that most of the commands are the same codes that you are using more frequently again and again. Taking %run as an example, which you are running:

%run One/Two/three/calculate_script.py

Assuming it ran successfully, you proceed to look over the results of the script and you see that there is an error in the calculations. After tracing the exact issue and once you have modified the calculate_script.py, you are free to search for the command by typing the letters contained in it, %run in this case, and press < Ctrl + P > or the < upward arrow > key to see the command history of those first matching for what you typed. You can navigate through the history pressing < Ctrl + P > or the < upward arrow > key as many times as necessary to find the command you were looking for and < Ctrl + N > or < downward arrow > in case you pass over the command you wanted to execute and need to come back. By repeatedly doing this it will become faster and most intuitive way to move in between commands.

Using < Ctrl + R > you can have the same incremental searching functionality from the readline used in UNIX-style shells, like in bash shells. The readline functionality in Windows is emulated by IPython. To use this utility, you can press < Ctrl + R > and then type a few characters from the input line you are looking for:

49

In [4]: a_command = foo(a, b, c)

(reverse-i-search) 'com': a_command = foo(a, b, c)

Then by pressing < Ctrl + R > you can jump to every line that matches with the exact characters typed by you.

Input and Output Variables

In case you forgot to assign the result of a function call to a variable, IPython has the solution. Both of the input (the text you provide in the input) and output (object that gets returned back) are stored in special variables.

For example:

In [7]: 3 ** 12

Out [7]: 531441

In [8]: _

Out [8]: 531441

You can find the stored input variables as _iX, meaning X as the input line number. There is an output variable _X corresponding to each input variable. So let's say that after input line 15, you'll see that there are two new variables; for the output named _15 and _i15 for the input.

In [14]: fun = 'car'

In [15]: fun

Out [15]: 'car'

In [16]: _i15
Out [16]: u'fun'

In [17]: _15
Out [17]: 'car'

You can execute the input variables again (as they are strings) with the Python exec keyword:

In [18]: exec _i15

There are a lot of magic functions that help you in using the input, as well as output, history. A function like %reset will help to delete all the variable names present in the namespace and is optional to remove stored input/output cache. You can also print the command history using %hist. And you can remove all references to a particular object from IPython using the %xdel function.

Logging the Input and Output

IPython allows you to log the complete console session, which includes the input as well as output. You can turn on logs by using the command %logstart.

For example:
In [8]: %logstart

You can record your complete session, which includes previous commands by enabling IPython logging at any point. This way, you can simply enable logging and save everything that has been done.

For more options, you can see the docstring of %logstart. It includes changing the path of output file.

Interacting with OS

IPython also provides a tight integration with the OS shell. Thanks to this useful feature, you are allowed to perform basic command line actions just as you would in other shells, such as the ones from Windows or UNIX without any need to exit from IPython. This means you can do things as change directories, execute shell commands and store the command's results in an IPython object such as a string or a list.

In below table you can find more information on magic functions.

Command	Description
%bookmark	To take advantage of bookmarking system of IPython's directory
!cmd	T execute cmd in shell
%pwd	To show the current system directory
%popd	To change directory to the start of the stack
%cd directory	To change the current working directory in system
Output = ! cmd args	To run cmd and store output of stdout
%dhist	To look up the history of directories

Shell Commands and Aliases

By starting a line with an exclamation point (!) or a bang, you are asking IPython to execute all code after the nag in the system shell. It implies that you have the power for changing directories, deleting files or executing any system related process. So you can even execute a process that will be taking away control from IPython, including another Python interpreter.

In [5]: !python
>>>

Dy allocating the !-cacapcd expression to u vuriuble, you can store the console output in any variable. For example, you can store the IP address of your Linux computer in a Python variable that is connected to internet.

In [6]: ip_value = !ifconfig eth0 | grep "inet "

In [7]: ip_value[0].strip()
Out [7]: 'inet addr:168.170.1.126 Bcast:168.170.1.255 Mask:255.255.255.0'

ip_value is a custom list type returned python object that contains different versions of the console input.

You can usc ! in IPython to substitute Python values, which are defined in the current environment. In order to achieve this, type the dollar sign $ before the variable name:

In [8]: fun = 'example*'

In [9]: !ls $fun

example9.py example.py example.xml

To define any custom shortcut for a particular shell command, you can use the %alias function. For example:

In [10]: %alias 13 ls -1

In [11]: 13 / usr

total 58

You can execute multiple commands by using semicolons to separate them.

In [12]: %alias alias_test (cd chapter02; ls; cd ..)

In [13]: alias_test

one.csv   two.csv   three.csv

Once the session is terminated, the aliases that you have defined earlier will also be removed in IPython. In case you have to create permanent aliases, you will need to change it in configuration system.

Directory Bookmark System

The directory bookmarking system in IPython helps you to save the aliases for common directories. That way, it will be easy to jump around them. As an example you can take Google mailbox and define a bookmark to help you to change directories to it:

In [1]: %bookmark data /project//GoogleMailbox/

Once this is done, you can use the %cd magic to use the bookmarks that you have already defined.

In [2]: cd data

(bookmark:data) -> /project//GoogleMailbox/

/project//GoogleMailbox/

In case any bookmark name becomes conflicted with an already existing directory name in the present working directory, you can override the bookmark location using the -b flag. To see all your defined bookmarks, you can use the -l option with %bookmark.

Now let us see an example:
In [3]: %bookmark -l
Current bookmarks:
data -> /project//GoogleMailbox/

In case of bookmarks, contrary to the aliases, they are automatically conserved between IPython sessions.

Software Development Tools

IPython not only offers a comfortable environment for data analysis and interactive GUI computing offered, but is widely considered as a perfect programming platform for software development. It's very important in data analysis that you have the right code as the first step. That's why IPython has a built-in Python pdb debugger, which is tightly integrated with IPython. Certainly you'll also look for a faster code to get the best results in data analysis. So simple-to-use code timing and profiling tools have been implemented in IPython. Here you'll find a more detailed overview on all the tools.

Interactive Debugger

The enhanced IPython's debugger provides more advantages to pdb with syntax highlighter, automatic tab completion, and line context in exception tracebacks. Code debugging comes in handy after an error has appeared in the program. Right after an exception, you can use the %debug command to call the debugger directly and open the full stack frame from the position where the exception was found:

In [3]: run chapter02/ipython_error.py

```
---------------------------------------------------------------------------
AssertionError Traceback (most recent call last)
/home/project/chapter02/ipython_error.py in <module>()
17 throws_an_exception()
18
---> 19 method_called()
```

/home/project/chapter02/ipython_error.py in method_called()

15 def method_called():

16 correct_working()

---> 17 throws_an_exception()

18

19 method_called()

/home/project/chapter02/ipython_error.py in throws_an_exception()

11 x = 2

12 y = 4

----> 13 assert(x + y == 8)

14

15 def method_called().

AssertionError:

In [4]: %debug

> /home/project/chapter02/ipython_error.py(13)

throws_an_exception()

12 y = 4

----> 13 assert(x + y == 8)

14

ipdb>

In order to look all the objects and data that are currently active in the interpreter inside the stack frame, you can arbitrarily execute IPython code from the debugger. It starts you in the lowest level by default right where the error occurred. In order to switch among various levels of the stack trace, you can do it by either pressing the u key(upwards) or the d key(downwards):

ipdb> u

> /home/project/chapter02/ipython_error.py(13) method_called()

16 correct_working()

---> 17 throws_an_exception()

18

Many users find this really useful because of the fact that you can automatically make the debugger window start by using the %pdb command after any exception has occurred in the program.

When you wish to set the breakpoints in your code to check the execution of any particular function so that you can examine the state of every variable at any stage, the debugger tool will help you a lot. You can do it in many ways. One way is to use the %run command suffixed with the -d character. This will invoke the debugger at the initial stage itself before running the code of the script. Once it is done, you need to use the (s) key to start the execution of your script:

In [6]: run -d chapter02/ipython_error.py

Breakpoint 1 at /home/project/chapter02/ipython_error.py:1

Note: Press 'c' at the ipdb> prompt to run the script.

> <string>(1)<module>()

ipdb> s

-- Call --

> /home/project/chapter02/ipython_error.py(1)<module>()

1---> 1 def correct_working():

2 x = 2

3 y = 4

From this point, you decide the way you want to work over the file. For instance, in the above mentioned example, you can set a breakpoint before calling the correct_working method. Then afterwards you can run the complete script by using the (c) key until it reaches the set breakpoint.

Now let us see an example:

ipdb> y 12

ipdb> c

> /home/project/chapter02/ipython_error.py(15) method_called()

14 def method_called():

2 --> 15 correct_working()

16 throws_an_exception()

So now you can press (n) key to step into correct_working() or run the correct_working() and move towards the next line.

You can advance to the line containing the error and check out the variables that are in the internal scope of the program by using throws_an_exception. Remember to use the prefix ! before the variables in order to look out their content. This prefix is required because the debugger command can automatically take precedence over those variable names.

Now let us see an example:

ipdb> s

-- Call --

> /home/project/chapter02/ipython_error.py(5)

throws_an_exception()

```
4
---- > 5 def throws_an_exception():
6 x = 2
ipdb> n
> //home/project/chapter02/ipython_error.py(6)
throws_an_exception()
5 def throws_an_exception():
----> 6 x = 2
7 y = 4
ipdb> n
> //home/project/chapter02/ipython_error.py(7)
throws_an_exception()
6 x = 2
---- > 7 y = 4
8 assert( x + y == 8)
ipdb> n
> /home/project/chapter02/ipython_error.py(8)
throws_an_exception()
7 y = 4
---- > 8 assert( x + y == 8)
9
ipdb> !x
2
ipdb> !y
4
```

Practice and experience is the most reliable way to become efficient when using the interactive debugger. You can also find a full list of the debugger commands in the below table. To anyone who is using the IDE for the first time, this debugger will look like a little bit difficult to start off with but along with time it will become easier.

Command	Description
H	It is used to show the command list
Help	It is used to provide the documentation for commands
C	It is used to resume the current program execution
B	It is used to set a particular breakpoint in the current program file
Q	It is used to exit from the debugger without further executing the program code
S	It is used to step inside a function call
N	It is used to run the current line and then move towards the next line in the program level
u or d	It is used to move upwards or downwards when inside a function call stack
A	It is used to display the arguments present inside the currently running function
debug	It is used to invoke the statement in an all new debugger
W	It is used to show the complete stack trace along with the context present at the current position
L	It is used to display the current position and the context that is at the current stack level

Ways to Use the Debugger

You can invoke the debugger with many other ways. One way is to call the set_trace() function. Here is how you can use it easily in your program:

```
def set_trace():
from IPython.core.debugger import Pdb
Pdb(color_scheme = 'Linux').set_trace(sys._getframe().f_back)

def debug(val, *args, **kwargs):
from IPython.core.debugger import Pdb
pdb = Pdb(color_scheme = 'Linux')
return pdb.runcall(val, *args, **kwargs)
```

It is very simple to use the set_trace() function. You can put the function anywhere in your program's code where you want it to get stopped. Then you can easily look around it; like for example, putting it before an exception has occured:

```
In [ 8 ]: run Chapter02/ipython_error.py
> /home/project/chapter02/ipython_error.py(15)method_called()
14 set_trace()
--- > 15 throws_an_exception()
16
```

Now you can easily use the (c) key to resume the code from where it stopped without any issues. You can also use the debug function defined above to invoke the debugger on any random function call.

```
def val(a, b, c = 1 ):
tempVal = a + b
return tempVal / c
```

Now you want to step into it to check the logic you have used in the code. If you use the function val() ordinarily it will look like val(1, 2, c=3). Therefore, if you wish to instead step into val directly, you need to pass val as the first argument to the debug function. After that pass the positional and the keyword arguments.

Now let us see an example:
```
In [ 9 ]: debug(val, 1, 2, c = 3)
> <ipython-input>(2)val()
2 def val(a, b, c):
---- > 3 tempVal = a + b
4 return tempVal / c
ipdb>
```

You can save a lot of time by using both the above code snippets on a regular basis.

You can also use the command %run in concurrence with the debugger. To do so, you have to execute the script suffixed by –d. That way you will get into the debugger console directly, set any breakpoints wherever you want in the code and run the script.

```
In [ 2 ]: %run -d chapter02/ipython_error.py
Breakpoint 1 at /home/project/chapter02/ipython_error.py:1
Note: Enter 'c' at the ipdb > prompt to run your script.
```

> <string>(1)<module>()

ipdb>

To start the debugger with a breakpoint that is already set by you, use –b along with a line number in your code.

```
In [ 3 ]: %run -d -b2 chapter02/ipython_error.py
Breakpoint 1 at /home/project/chapter02/ipython_error.py:2
Note: Enter 'c' at the ipdb > prompt to run your script.
> <string>(1)<module>()
ipdb> c
> /home/project/chapter02/ipython_error.py(2)correct_working()
1 def correct_working():
1 --- > 3 x = 2
4 y = 4
ipdb>
```

Calculate Execution Time

Sometimes it is very important to know the execution time of the individual function calls or code statements; especially when you are working on a large-scale application that has large amount of data and processing involved in it. It comes in handy as you will get to know which functions defined by you are taking a lot of execution time. To help you with this, IPython provides you with the in-built commands to check your code's execution time easily.

You won't like to use the in-built time module to check your execution time as it is very repetitive and tedious task. Its function time.clock() is not used much now because of the same reason.

IPython has two in-built functions to automate the above problem for you. They are: %time and %timeit.

%time will check the statement one at a time by running it and then gives youthe total execution time. For example, you are having relatively huge list of strings and you want to know the performance timing of different methods to select the strings that start with a prefix specified by you.

Here is a list of 5,00,000 strings and two similar methods to perform the above logic for the strings starting with the prefix 'book'.

```
# Huge list of 5 lakh strings
allStrings = [ 'book', 'notebook', 'pen', 'school', 'teacher' ] * 100000
firstMethod = [ i for i in strings if i.startswith('book') ]
secondMethod = [ i for i in strings if i[:4] == 'book']
```

You will think that both will have the same execution time. We can check it using the %time command:

In [243]: %time firstMethod = [i for i in strings if i.startswith('book')]

CPU times: user 0.15 s, sys: 0.00 s, total: 0.15 s

Wall time: 0.15 s

In [244]: %time secondMethod = [i for i in strings if i[:4] == 'book']

CPU times: user 0.07 s, sys: 0.00 s, total: 0.07 s

Wall time: 0.07 s

Here the Wall time is the main thing to be considered. Therefore, as per the above wall time, we can see that the firstMethod took twice as much time as the secondMethod. But it is not actually the precise timing. You can check it yourself by running the above codes again and again; you will notice that the results are not always the same. Therefore, in order to have a precise and accurate timing, we need to use the %timeit command. When we provide any random statement to %timeit, it will run the statement multiple times to provide a fairly precise execution time.

In [245]: %timeit [i for i in strings if i.startswith('book')]
10 loops, best of 2: 068 ms per loop
In [246]: %timeit [i for i in strings if i[:4] == 'book']
10 loops, best of 2: 641 ms per loop

This example illustrates the importance of Python's standard library functions to check your code's performance. Libraries like pandas and NumPy are really helpful in performance management in the large scale applications where every millisecond matters.

%timeit comes in handy when you want to analyze the functions and statements having very little execution time. It can give you detailed results from microseconds to nanoseconds. When you have any function that gets called a million times, these microseconds will add up together to have a difference of seconds or even minutes in your overall data analysis timing. Let's see the below example:

In [247]: a = 'book'
In [248]: b = 'books'
In [249]: %timeit a.startswith(b)
1000000 loops, best of 2: 893 ns per loop
In [250]: %timeit a[:4] == b
10000000 loops, best of 2: 784 ns per loop

Profiling Code

Profiling code is also related to the code's execution timing except for the fact that it determines where the time is spent. The main profiling tool used in Python is called cProfile. Please note that it is not related to IPython. cProfile helps to execute blocks of code or the complete program and keeps track of time spent on every function present in the program.

You can use cProfile on command line by running the complete program and then getting the combined time per function as output.

You can run the below script via cProfile in command line:
python -m cProfile own_example.py

Once you run that, you will see the execution time for all functions sorted by their names in ascending order. It can be pretty difficult to check where the most time has been actually spent. To overcome this, you can use sort order by using –s suffux after cProfile command.

For example:
$ python -m cProfile -s cumulative own_example.py
One with the most time: 9.12572475
21376 function calls (17534 primitive calls) in 1.32 seconds

One thing to note here is that if a function calls another function, its timing will not stop there. It will calculate the total time required by the function until it exits from it. It will record the start time and the end time to give you the results.

cProfile not only provides the above command line function, but it can also be used to profile any code blocks without the need to start a new process. IPython provides a suitable interface with %prun command.

In [251]: %prun -l 8 -s cumulative own_example()
6932 function calls in 0.738 seconds

The above approach by calling %run –p -s provides the same feature, but you won't have to exit the IPython interface.

Profiling a Function Line-by-Line

When %prun does not show you the entire executing time from a function or it shows you results that are hard to read, like complex outputs arranged by function names, you can run a small library named line_profiler, which can be obtained from PyPI as well as package management tools.

Line_profiler has an in-built function named %lprun that has the capability to execute the line by line profiling for the functions present in your program. In order to have access to this in-built function, you have to modify your IPython configuration by adding this line:

c.TerminalIPythonApp.extensions = ['line_profiler']

Although line_profiler can be used for programming, it will work in a much better and faster way when combined with IPython.

As soon as you have activated the line_profiler extension in IPython, a new command %lprun will also be available for use. The basic difference in using both of them is that you need to specify the functions to be included while using %lprun. Here is the syntax:

%lprun -f firstFunction -f secondFunction **statement_to_profile**

For "macro" profiling it is advisable to run %prun (cProfile) and for "micro" profiling %lprun (line_profiling) is the best choice.

IPython HTML Notebook

IPython Notebook was launched in 2011 by Brian Granger. He wanted to build a web technology that was based on the model of research and teaching. From then, it has grown immensely as an interactive computing tool for data analysis and interpretation. It consists of a JSON based ipynb doc format. This format helps to share the code, figures, and output easily. The IPython Notebook application is a very lightweight process that runs on the command line.

To start IPython Notebook, you can use the below commands:
$ ipython notebook --pylab=inline
[NotebookApp] Using existing profile dir:
                u'/home/project/.config/ipython/profile_default'
[NotebookApp] Serving notebooks from
                /home/project/large_scripts
[NotebookApp] IPython Notebook is running at:
                http://168.0.0.1:8888/
[NotebookApp] Use Control-C to stop this server and shut down all kernels.

In most of the platforms, the primary web browser in your system will open up the notebook dashboard on its own. In rare cases, you might need to open the URL on your own and then create a notebook there to start the process.

As the notebook is being used inside your primary web browser, you can run the server process anywhere.

Chapter 3

Introduction to Pandas

What is Python Programming Language?

Python is an object Oriented, interpreted programming language. It helps in faster development as it is an interpreted language (which makes it a scripting language as well) and does not need compilation. One of most popular uses of Python is for data analysis. Data Scientists want to visualize data to convey their analysis results.

Python is a dynamically typed and dynamically bind language.

Dynamically Typed: We do not need to initialize variables beforehand.

Dynamic Binding: Links procedure calls to method at run time.

Introduction to Pandas

Pandas is a package used in python for analyzing data. Pandas is one of the most widely used tool in data munging/wrangling (process of transforming and mapping data from raw data form into another more appropriate and valuable form, which can be used for downstream purpose such as analytics). Pandas is open source, free to use (under a BSD license) and was originally written by Wes McKinney. Pandas takes data (from CSV file or SQL database) and convert it into python objects in the form of rows and columns (here you can imagine it as a table).

In Python, Pandas is an open source library that is responsible for delivering high performance as well as usable data structures. It is a BSD licensed library that provides the required data analysis tools within the platform of Python. Primarily, the Pandas library enables faster data analysis in Python. Pandas library is appropriate to be used in the applications that are built on NumPy because Pandas itself is built on the NumPy library.

Pandas is a package used in Python to make analysis of relational database (such as SQL) and labeled data (excel, csv) easy, fast and intuitive. Examples where Pandas can be Used for data analytics are:
- Read/Write JSON with Pandas
- Read/Write Excel with Pandas
- Read/Write CSV with Pandas

Why Pandas library is important

Pandas library can be used for a specific set of analysis requirements for a given data. Some of those will be:

- Data structures that have labeled axes, support the automatic alignment of data. Explicit or automatic alignment prevent some of the errors that might arise from misalignment of the data. This also prevents errors that might arise from data that has been differently indexed or might from multiple sources.

- Integration of the time series (association of value points with time) functionality.

- The given data structures should be capable of handling both the time-series data as well as the non-time series data.

- Handling of the missing data with much need flexibility.

- Easy passage of the metadata that would have resulted from any arithmetic operations or any form of reduction operations.

- Can use a host of relational operations, including merge on a given set of data. The relational operations are found in legacy databases such as SQL.

The Pandas library in Python meet these requirements, and that is why it is considered as one of the important resources in Python. It is easy to use and is perfectly suited for generic software development. Even though Python used to be one of the best programming languages for software development, initially, it didn't have the collection of tools and the data structures, which can fulfill the above-mentioned functionalities. But this was very much possible with the integration of the Pandas library with Python.

Pandas did provide much-needed data structures and tools to Python, which can be used for the swift analysis of data.

Installation and Getting Started

In order to use pandas, one would need to install it first. You would also need to have Python 2.7 and above as a pre-requirement for installation. The easiest way to install pandas is installing it through a package like Anaconda Distribution (a platform for data analysis and scientific computing).

Please find below link for instructions to install pandas
http://pandas.pydata.org/pandas-docs/stable/install.html

Import pandas and NumPy libraries;
In [4]: import pandas as pd
        Import numpy as np

Generally, you would add "as pd" (or "as np") alias, so you can access different commands as "pd.command" instead of "pandas.command" saving you from typing more characters.

From the above code, we can see that Pandas library is being imported as "pd". So, whenever, the word "pd" is seen within a code, one needs to understand that it is a direct reference to the Pandas library. Since we use DataFrame and Series quite often, it will be a good idea to import them to the local namespace. The above code does exactly the same.

Let's Start Working!

We can code our program in different IDEs like Jupyter, Spyder, which come along with the Anaconda package.

We can use pandas with other libraries like NumPy, MatPlotLib, SKlearn for data analysis and visualization purpose. Pandas is a powerful and simplicity data analysis framework for Python. It's tightly incorporated with NumPy and matplotlib packages.

The Pandas library has evolved incrementally in last four years and has developed itself into a much broader and a larger library. The well-developed Pandas library can now handle complex problems related to the data analysis, with the simplicity it is known for. That has been the beauty of Pandas; it still exists with the ease-of-use even though as a library it has grown over these years. For a programmer, it means a lot since he desires for a platform that is simple as well as easy to use, with lots of utilities. At the end of this book, one can easily understand the reason why Pandas is considered as one of the important components of Python. In the rest of this book, we will use the common conventions for import in Pandas. The import conventions are mentioned below.

Note: All the coding is performed in Jupyter Notebook using python 3 kernel.

Loading and Saving Data with Pandas

We have already mentioned that Pandas is simple and it is easy to use. However, one needs to be familiar with two of the most important data structures in Pandas.

Basically, there are two primary data structure with Pandas:
1. Pandas series (1-D array)
2. Pandas Dataframes (2-D array)

While we progress through this book, we will discuss more of these. Both of them are not a one-stop solution for any of the problems you might encounter in Python, but they do provide a robust as well easy to use platform for the majority of the applications.

A "Series" in Pandas can be described as an object, that is a unidimensional array. This array contains data, of the data type NumPy. It also contains another array that is made up of data labels and is referred to as an index. The simplest format of Series is created with a single array of data. This has been shown below.

If one carefully notes the representation of the strings in the above example, it is quite interesting as well as interactive. In the given string, we can see that the index is located on the left while the value is located on the right. Interestingly, we never specified an index for a given data. Hence, a default index number is assigned to the values. The index value ranges from 0 to N-1, where N denotes the length of the given data. One can easily get the representation of the Array along with the index object of the given Series, through the values of the attributes & index respectively. This has been demonstrated in the code below.

It is always recommended that one should always create a Series, with each of the data point having an index. This is definitely one of the best practices.

In case you are selecting a single value or a specific set of values, you can always use the values that are in the index. This is something that is not possible in the normal NumPy array.

When you perform certain types of operations on NumPy arrays, such as scalar multiplication, application of math functions or even applying a filter on a Boolean array, the index-value reference or the link will be preserved. This is demonstrated in the code below.

A Series can be also referenced as an ordered dict with a fixed length since it maps the index values to the given set of data values. Hence, Series can substitute several functions that might have been expecting a dict.

You can actually create a Series by passing a dict, only if that Python dict contains data.

As you pass on the dict, the index in the newly creates Series will have the keys of the dict in sorted order.

You can have multiple sources of data such as excel, CSV file, text file, website links, SQL database. We can read file with command:

pd.read_filetype

Here filetype part will change in accordance with filetype where your data is residing.

Example:
pd.read_csv()
pd.read_excel()
pd.read_html()
pd.read_sql()

How to read a .csv file?

```
        import pandas as p
        path = 'D:\\Python\\marysoloman\\new\\'
dfl = p.read_csv(path + 'test.csv')
dfl
```

Explanation:
import is required since pandas is a package.

Import pandas as p is an alias.

df(dataframes) is a data structure of pandas used to store the data of the file.

Read_csv(path+filename): to read csv file (other methods: read_excel, read_sql, etc.)

Dfl is used to display all the values stored in dataframe

Other Related Commands:
df.head()-To view top 5 values of a file

df.tail()- To view bottom 5 values of file

We will import famous IRIS data from excel file.

It's always good practice to have a quick view of data using *head* command

How to read values of a single column?

```
import pandas as p
df1 = p.read_csv("D:\\Python\\marysoloman\\new\\test.csv',
index_col = False)
QI = df1['QID']
print(QI)
```

Explanation:

QI is a variable name where we are storing the value

df['QID']-> 'QID' is name of column header

Case 1:

If you want to retrieve two or more columns and save it in dataframe structure for further use you can add the following:

```
import pandas as p
df1 =
p.read_csv('C:\\Users\\akanksha.amarendra\\Desktop\\new\\test.csv'
, index_col=False)
df1 = df1[['QID','Category']]
df1
```

Case 2:

In case you want conditions on rows and well as columns:

    a)   all rows and selected columns

```
import pandas as p
```

```
df1 =
p.read_csv("D:\\Python\\marysoloman\\new\\test.csv',index_col =
False)
df1 = df1.loc[:,['QID','Category']]
df1
```

b) selected rows and selected columns

```
import pandas as p
df1 = p.read_csv("D:\\Python\\marysoloman\\new\\test.csv',
index_col = False)
df1 = df1.loc[[1,2],['QID','Category']]
df1
```

How to retrieve a particular value from a column?

```
import pandas as p
df1 = p.read_csv("D:\\Python\\marysoloman\\new\\test.csv',
index_col = False)
Qi = df1['QID'].values[0]
print(Qi)
```

Explanation:

-Qi is a variable

-df1.['QID'].values[0]-> used to retrieve data from QID column at 0th index

-"index_col = False" -> in path is to remove the serial number column that would have otherwise been displayed with the "Qi"

How to save the value retrieved in a text file?

```
import pandas as p
df1 = p.read_csv("D:\\Python\\marysoloman\\new\\test.csv',
index_col = False)
Qi = df1['QID'].values[0]
with open("D:\\Python\\marysoloman\\new\\.txt', 'w') as f:
f.write("QID %d" % Qi)
```

Explanation:

The value can be stored in text file using the highlighted part of code.

How to save multiple values in multiple files?

```
import pandas as p
 path = "D:\\Python\\marysoloman\\new\\'
 df1 = p.read_csv("D:\\Python\\marysoloman\\new\\test.csv',
index_col = False)
 for i in range(0,
len(open("D:\\Python\\marysoloman\\new\\test.csv').readlines())):
   Qid = df1['QID'].values[i]
   category = df1['Category'].values[i]
   dest_path = path + category + str(Qi) + str(i)
   with open(dest_path + '.txt', 'w') as f:
     f.write("QID %d" % Qid + "\n")
     f.write("Category %s" % category)
```

Explanation:

-len(open(path).readlines())) is used to get the length of the file

-values[i] read entire value and save it into file.

Note: If the column value ahas special character like [/ , % *] the file will not be saved, make sure you replace all the special characters beforehand.

How to group the data as per column values?

df = p.read_csv("D:\\Python\\marysoloman\\new\\test.csv")

path = "D:\\Python\\marysoloman\\new\\'

for name, group in df.groupby('QID'):

  # print the name of the regiment

  group.to_csv(path + name.astype(str) + '.csv')

Explanation:

Name in for loop will be the QID received from the file

df.groupby('column_name') used to group the data by QID.

group.to_csv(path) used to save file at particular path with name in csv format.

name.astype(str) is used because value of name i.e. QID is Integer.

Python Pandas DataFrame

It is basically a 2-D data structure having columns of different types. It acts as like a Microsoft Excel spreadsheet as well as a SQL database table. It has the capability to accept various types of data input like the below ones:

- Structured ndarray
- DataFrame
- Dict of 1D ndarrays, dicts, Series, or lists
- A Series
- 2-D numpy.ndarray

When using pandas, we must import the following:

import pandas as pd

Creating a DataFrame

import pandas as pd

df = pd.DataFrame({ 'A' : [21, 22, 23, 42],
'B' : [24, 23, 22, 13],
'C' : [67, 14, 12, 18],
'D' : [24, 53, 52, 41] })
print df

The below outcome shows the DataFrame creation with the different columns.

```
   A  B  C  D
0 21 24 67 24
1 22 23 14 53
2 23 22 12 52
3 42 13 18 41
```

Column Selection, Addition, Deletion

User can select, add and delete the columns in DataFrame like a SQL table operation.

Selection

We can select specific or all columns from DataFrame, as shown below.

Example - Selection:

```
import pandas as pd
df = pd.DataFrame( { 'A' : [21, 22, 23, 42],
                     'B' : [24, 23, 22, 13],
                     'C' : [67, 14, 12, 18],
                     'D' : [24, 53, 52, 41] } )
print df['A']
```

Output:

```
0    21
1    22
2    23
3    42
Name: A, dtype: int64
```

Addition:

We can add specific columns to DataFrame, as shown below.

Example - Addition:

```
import pandas as pd
df = pd.DataFrame( { 'A' : [21, 22, 23, 42],
                     'B' : [24, 23, 22, 13],
                     'C' : [67, 14, 12, 18],
                     'D' : [24, 53, 52, 41] } )
df[ 'E' ] = df[ 'A' ] * df[ 'B' ]
print df
```

Output:

```
    A   B   C   D   E
0  21  24  67  24  504
1  22  23  14  53  506
2  23  22  12  52  506
3  42  13  18  41  546
```

Deletion

Columns can be deleted or popped from DataFrame.
Example:

```
import pandas as pd
df = pd.DataFrame( { 'A' : [21, 22, 23, 42],
                     'B' : [24, 23, 22, 13],
                     'C' : [67, 14, 12, 18],
                     'D' : [24, 53, 52, 41] } )
# Delete the column
del df[ 'A' ]

# Pop the column
df.pop( 'B' )

print df
```

Output:

```
    C   D
0  67  24
1  14  53
2  12  52
3  18  41
```

DataFrame - Insert Column:

It's used to insert at a specific location in the columns. By default, the columns are inserted at the end.

Example:

```
import pandas as pd
df = pd.DataFrame( { 'A' : [21, 22, 23, 42],
                     'B' : [24, 23, 22, 13],
                     'C' : [67, 14, 12, 18],
                     'D' : [24, 53, 52, 41] } )
df.insert(1, 'E', df[ 'A' ])
print df
```

Output:

```
   A   E   B   C   D
0  21  21  24  67  24
1  22  22  23  14  53
2  23  23  22  12  52
3  42  42  13  18  41
```

DataFrame - Indexing, Selection

Row selection, it returns a *Series* result whose index is the columns of the DataFrame.

Now let us see an example:

```
import pandas as pd
df = pd.DataFrame( { 'A' : [21, 22, 23, 42],
                     'B' : [24, 23, 22, 13],
                     'C' : [67, 14, 12, 18],
                     'D' : [24, 53, 52, 41] } )
```

print "\nActual DataFrame: \n", df

print "\nZero(0) Location Index Result: \n",df.loc[0]

print "\nZero(0) Location Index Result: \n", df.iloc[0]

Output:

Actual DataFrame:

```
   A   B   C   D
0  21  24  67  24
1  22  23  14  53
2  23  22  12  52
3  42  13  18  41
```

Zero (0) Location Index Result:

```
A   21
B   24
C   67
D   24
```

Zero (0) Location Index Result:

```
A   21
B   24
C   67
D   24
```

DataFrame - Transpose

We use T attribute when we need to transform data from row-level to columnar data.

Now let us see an example:

```
import pandas as pd
df = pd.DataFrame( { 'A' : [21, 22, 23, 42],
                     'B' : [24, 23, 22, 13],
                     'C' : [67, 14, 12, 18],
                     'D' : [24, 53, 52, 41] } )
print "Actual DataFrame : \n", df
print "\nAfter Transpose : \n", df.T
```

Output:

```
Actual DataFrame:
   A   B   C   D
0  21  24  67  24
1  22  23  14  53
2  23  22  12  52
3  42  13  18  41

After Transpose:
   0   1   2   3
A  21  22  23  42
B  24  23  22  13
C  67  14  12  18
D  24  53  52  41
```

DataFrame - Groupby

It is used to arrange identical data into groups. We could naturally group by either single column or list of columns.

Example:

```
import pandas as pd
import numpy as np

df = pd.DataFrame({'A' : ['fo', 'ba', 'fo', 'ba','fo', 'ba', 'fo', 'fo'],
'B' : ['one', 'one', 'two', 'three', 'two', 'two', 'one', 'three'],
'C' : np.random.randn(8),
'D' : np.random.randn(8)})
grouped – df.groupby('A')
print grouped.groups
```

Output:

```
{'fo': [0L, 2L, 4L, 6L, 7L], 'ba': [1L, 3L, 5L]}
```

DataFrame - Iterating through Grouped Data

Iterating through the grouped data is similarly iterating the normal for loop.

Now let us see an example:

```
import pandas as pd
import numpy as np
df = pd.DataFrame({'A' : ['fo', 'ba', 'fo', 'ba','fo', 'ba', 'fo', 'fo'],
'B' : ['one', 'one', 'two', 'three', 'two', 'two', 'one', 'three'],
'C' : np.random.randn(8),
'D' : np.random.randn(8)})
```

```
grouped = df.groupby('A')
for name, group in grouped:
        print name, group
```

Output:
```
ba    A    B      C         D
1 ba   one 0.286725 0.735988
3 ba three 0.031028 1.368286
5 ba   two -0.095358 -0.466581


fo    A    B      C         D
0 fo   one -0.168500 0.155344
2 fo   two 0.234364 1.336054
4 fo   two -0.397370 0.722332
6 fo   one 0.714563 -1.437803
7 fo three -1.307215 -0.118485
```

DataFrame – Aggregation

Once the Groupby is complete, various methods are available to do a computation on the grouped data. The method name as below.

        aggregate or agg

Now let us see an example:
```
import pandas as pd
import numpy as np
df = pd.DataFrame({'A' : ['fo', 'ba', 'fo', 'ba','fo', 'ba', 'fo', 'fo'],
'B' : ['one', 'one', 'two', 'three', 'two', 'two', 'one', 'three'],
'C' : np.random.randn(8),
'D' : np.random.randn(8)})
```

```
grouped = df.groupby('A')
print grouped.aggregate(np.sum)
```

Output:

```
A         C         D
ba  0.282556 -0.368244
fo -1.434853 -4.828347
A         C         D
ba  0.282556 -0.368244
fo -1.434853 -4.828347
```

Applying Multiple Functions at Once

With grouped data we can pass a list of functions to do an aggregation. It returns DataFrame as outcome.

Now let us see an example:

```
import pandas as pd
import numpy as np
df = pd.DataFrame({'A' : ['fo', 'ba', 'fo', 'ba','fo', 'ba', 'fo', 'fo'],
'B' : ['one', 'one', 'two', 'three','two', 'two', 'one', 'three'],
'C' : np.random.randn(8),
'D' : np.random.randn(8)})
grouped = df.groupby(['A','B'])
print grouped.agg(['sum','mean'])
```

Output:

A	B	C		D	
		sum	mean	sum	mean
ba	one	1.900910	1.900910	0.887157	0.887157
	three	-0.668119	-0.668119	1.387096	1.387096
	two	-0.311151	-0.311151	1.492372	1.492372

fo	one	-0.247782	-0.123891	0.057516	0.028758
	three	0.098512	0.098512	1.595713	1.595713
	two	2.342468	1.171234	1.897002	0.948501

Important Functionalities

We will see the basic and important mechanisms of data interaction in DataFrame and series in this section. We will not focus on all the documentation present in the pandas library; but instead we will see the most important and frequently used functionalities.

Re-indexing

An important function to perform on pandas objects is to re-index. It is a process in which we create a new object and the data follows to the new index. Let us see an example:

In [1]: first_obj = Series([2.4, 5.1, 3.7, 7.6], index = ['v', 'u', 'w', 'x'])
In [2]: first_obj
Out [2]:
v 2.4
u 5.1
w 3.7
x 7.6

Now we will call the reindex function on the first object. It will rearrange all the data as per the new index.

In [3]: new_obj = obj.reindex(['u', 'v', 'w', 'x', 'y'])

In [4]: new_obj

Out [4]:

u 5.1

v 2.4

w 3.7

x 7.6

y NaN

We can also set the missing values to 0 if we use the fill_value argument inside the function.

In [5]: newobj.reindex(['u', 'v', 'w', 'x', 'y'], fill_value = 0)

Out[5]:

u 5.1

v 2.4

w 3.7

x 7.6

y 0.0

We can also use the arguments ffill and bfill to carry values forward or carry values backwards, respectively.

Here are some of the arguments that can be used with the reindex function.

Argument name	Description of the argument
Index	It is used to provide a new index sequence to the object. It will be used exactly the same in the new object.
Fill_value	It is used to replace the missing values in the newly re-indexed object with your own defined values. For example, you can replace it with 0.
Limit	It is used to fill the maximum size gap while filling it forward or backward.
Copy	It is used to command not to copy the underlying data in case both the new index and the old index are identical. Its default value is True, which means it will copy the data at all times.
Level	It is used to match the simple index if there are multiple index. If not, then it will select its subset.

Removing Entries from Axis

It is easier to drop one or multiple entries from the axis if we have a list or array index without the entries. It requires a little logic and munging. We can use the drop function, which returns the new object indicating the deleted values from the axis. Let us seen an example:

In [6]: first_obj = Series(np.arange(5.), index = ['u', 'v', 'w', 'x', 'y'])

In [7]: new_obj = first_obj.drop('w')

In [8]: new_obj

Out [8]:
u 0
v 1
x 3
y 4

In [9]: first_obj.drop(['x', 'w'])

Out [9]:
u 0
v 1
y 4

In case of DataFrame, we can delete the index values from either of the axis.

Let us see an example:
In [10]: obj_data = DataFrame(np.arange(9).reshape((3, 3)),
....: index = ['USA', 'UK', 'Canada'],
....: columns = ['first', 'second', 'third'])
In [11]: obj_data.drop(['UK', 'USA'])
Out [11]:

	First	second	third
Canada	6	7	8

Function Mapping

All the ufuncs in NumPy (array methods) can easily work with objects created in pandas.

In [12]: obj_frame = DataFrame(np.random.randn(4, 3), columns = list('xyz'),

.....:   index = ['USA', 'UK', 'Tokyo', 'Canada'])

In [13]: obj_frame

Out [13]:

	x	y	z
USA	0.1235	0.5248	0.5823
UK	1.7383	0.4629	0.2346
Tokyo	0.5683	0.3146	1.9424
Canada	1.626	-0.4245	0.9124

In [14]: np.abs(obj_frame)

Out [14]:

	x	y	z
USA	0.1235	0.5248	0.5823
UK	1.7383	0.4629	0.2346
Tokyo	0.5683	0.3146	1.9424
Canada	1.626	-0.4245	0.9124

One more operation is to apply a function to every row or column on a 1-Dimensional array. The apply() function present in DataFrame performs the exact task.

Most of the array methods used for calculations like the sum & mean of numbers are present in the DataFrame functions. Therefore, it is not required to use the apply method there.

It is not necessary that the apply function will return a scalar value only; it can be a series as well having multiple values in it.

In [15]: def fun(a):
.....: return Series([a.max(), a.min()], index = ['maximum', 'minimum'])
In [16]: obj_frame.apply(a)

Out[16]:

	x	y	z
minimum	-0.1395	0.1396	-0.3561
maximum	1.1435	0.9587	1.9465

Element wise Python functions can also be used here. We can use the applymap method. It has been named so because a map function is already there in series, which performs the same task.

Sorting in Pandas

Sorting is a process of arranging the row or column values systematically using some pre0defined criteria. It can be done on the row or the column index with the help of sort index function. It will return a new object with the sorted values.

Let us see an example.
In [17]: first_obj = Series(range(4), index = ['x', 'u', 'v', 'w'])

In [18]: first_obj.sort_index()

Out [18]:

u 1

v 2

w 3

x 0

We can sort the DataFrame by using both axis index.

In [19]: obj_frame = DataFrame(np.arange(8).reshape((2, 4)),
index = ['third', 'first'],

.....:   columns = ['x', 'u', 'v', 'w'])

In [20]: obj_frame.sort_index()

Out [20]:

	x	u	v	w
first	4	5	6	7
third	0	1	2	3

By default, the data is sorted in ascending value. If we want to sort it in the descending order, then we need to pass the argument ascending = False in the sort function.

In order to sort the Series, we can use the order function. If there are any missing values present in the Series, then by default it will be sorted at the end.

In [21]: first_obj = Series([3, 6, -2, 1])

In [22]: first_obj.order()

Out [22]:

2 -2

3 1

0 3

1 6

Chapter 4

NumPy Basics

Introduction

The NumPy, which is the short form of Numerical Python, is the core library for handling scientific computation in python related to arrays and vectorized computation. In this book, the base of all high-level tools is this library. In data analysis, data cleaning NumPy is most widely used library.

NumPy provides these features:

- Creating multidimensional array are represented as ndarray and are fast and methodical
- This library is also used in linear algebra, broadcasting, random number generation.
- It is convenient for reading and writing txt or similar files
- With the help of this library mathematical and statistical operations can be done easily
- Using this, python can wrap or integrate C, C++ codebases easily by sending data to external packages from low level codebase and it is dynamic and effortless C API
- It is used in array-oriented computing.

Though it is not widely used in complicated data analysis, if you want to use other python libraries like pandas, scikit-learn, tensorflow, you have to be fully aware of all the specification of NumPy library. The Broadcasting, an advanced feature of NumPy, is discussed later.

In this chapter, we will be focusing on following functionalities.

• Faster array operations like data cleaning & munging, filtering the data, transforming data, and many other computations.
• Basic algorithms related to array, such as sorting algorithms, set operations, and unique algorithms.
• Productive and well-structured descriptive statistics and data aggregation.
• Aligning the data and other relational data in order to merge or join the heterogeneous data-sets.
• Demonstrating the conditional logic for various array operations in place of loops having if-else statements.

In high level data analysis pandas are widely used, where NumPy is used only in mathematical computational level. Time series manipulation and many other features are only included in pandas. That's why in basic operations pandas are used.

Short Notes:

In most of the book, numpy is imported like this: import numpy as np. It can also be imported like, from numpy import *. But the first one is my recommended convention of importing array.

NumPy ndarray: A Multidimensional Array Object

In this subtopic, the ndarray is the full form of N-Dimensional array, which is fast, space efficient and flexible and is indexed by a tuple of non-negative integers. It is one of the key features. This gives you access to do mathematical and statistical operation easily. In this type of array homogeneous or same type of data are stored.

In [9]:   values
Out [9]:   array([[1.55, -1.14 , -1.23],   [0.39, 0.79, 0.14]])

In [10]:   values * 10
Out [10]:   array([[15.5, -11.4, -12.3],   [1.39, 7.9, 1.4]])

In [11]:   values + 1
Out [11]:   array([[2.55, -0.14 , -0.23],   [1.39, 1.79, 1.14]])

The .shape indicate the size of the array and .dtype object indicates the datatype of the array. The size of the array also be derived from len() method, which will give results as an integer as shown below.

In [12]:   values.shape
Out [12]:   (2, 3)

In [13]:   values.dtype
Out [13]:   dtype('float64')

This chapter will teach you the basic and utmost understanding of numpy features that will be first step to be proficient as a python programmer.

```
import numpy as np                    # It is the most widely used convention
                                       to import numpy

x = np.array( [ 10, 20, 30, 40 ] )    # This will create an array of rank 1

print(type(x))                         # This will print "<class
                                        'numpy.ndarray'>"

print(x.shape)                         # This will print "(4)"

print(a[0], a[1], a[2])                # This will print "10 20 30 40"

x[0] = 5                               # This will modify the first element
                                        present in the array

print(x)                               # This will print "[5, 20, 30, 40]"

print(x.ndin)                          # This will print "1"
```

Short Notes:

With little bit of exceptions, the ndarray, numpy array and array are similar as objects of numpy array.

Creating ndarrays

To create arrays in numpy we have to use .array functions. It works like following.

```
>>> x = np.array( [10 ,20, 30] )
>>> y = np.array([ (10, 20, 30), ( 40, 50, 60) ], dtype = int)
>>> z = np.array( [[( 10, 20, 30), ( 40, 50, 60) ], [ (30, 20, 10), ( 40, 50, 60) ]], dtype = int)
```

A list of equal-length lists, which is a Nested list, will get converted to a multidimensional array:

In [20]: values = [[10, 20, 30, 40], [50, 60, 70, 80]]

In [21]: array1 = np.array(values)

In [22]: array1
Out [22]: array ([[10, 20, 30, 40] , [50, 60, 70, 80]])

In [23]: array1.ndim
Out [23]: 2

In [24]: array1.shape
Out[24]: (2, 4)

In [25]: array1.dtype
Out [25]: dtype('int32')

There are many functions for creating arrays like ones and zeros and empty. For example, **arrange** is an in-built method used in the array value present in the range function.

In [27]: np.arange(20)

Out [27]: array ([20, 21, 22, 23, 24, 25, 26, 27, 28, 29, 30, 31, 32, 33, 34, 35, 36, 37, 38, 39, 40])

Below table has the list of some common functions used for array creation. As NumPy's main focus is on numerical computing, if the data type is not specified explicitly, it will be found as float in many cases. They work like below:

```
>>> np.zeros((2,3))                    # It helps in creating an array
                                         of all zeros

>>> np.ones((1,2,3), dtype = np.int16) # It helps in creating an array
                                         of all ones

>>> x = np.arange(5,10,18, 7)          # It helps in creating an array
                                         of evenly spaced values (which
                                         is step value)

>>> np.linspace(0,1,8)                 # It helps in creating an array
                                         of evenly spaced values (which
                                         is number of samples)

>>> y = np.full( (1, 1), 6)            # It helps in creating a constant
                                         array

>>> z = np.eye(3)                      # It helps in creating a 3 X 2
                                         identity matrix

>>> np.random.random( (3, 3) )         # It helps in creating an array
                                         with all the random values

>>> np.empty( (2,3) )                  # It helps in creating an empty
                                         array
```

Short Notes:

np.empty can give zeros or pre-initialized garbage value. So, use it with caution.

This is a short list of function that creates array, and the datatypes will be float64 if not pre-specified.

Function Name	Description of the function
array	It converts the input data like array, tuple, list into a ndarray. It is done either by specifying a dtype explicitly or by inferring a dtype. It will also by default copy the input data entered by you.
empty	It will create new arrays without any initial values and only allocates new memory to the array.
as array	It will convert the input data to a ndarray, but it will disregard it if the input provided by you is already a ndarray.
arrange	It is an in-built method used in the array value present in the range function. It will return the ndarray and not the list.
ones	It will create an array comprising of all 1's. It will take input for the shape and dtype of the array.
eye	It will produce a N x N matrix, which has all 1's in the diagonal and all 0's in the remaining matrix.

Data Types for ndarrays

The dtype or datatype is an object that contains the details of ndarray, which it needs to interpret. It makes NumPy compact and flexible in memory management. The numerical data types have similar names like float and int followed by the number, which is the number of bits per element.

```
>>> In [ 29 ]: x = np.array( [10, 20, 30 ] , dtype = np.int32 )
>>> In [ 30 ]: y = np.array( [10.57, 20.34, 30.84] , dtype = np.float64 )
>>> In [ 31 ]: x.dtype
>>> In [ 32 ]: y.dtype

>>> Out [ 31 ]: dtype('int32')
>>> Out [ 32 ]: dtype('float64')
```

NumPy can detect data types from input automatically. It works on machinery representation as a result numpy can interpret C/C++ code bases.

Here are some examples,
Complex
```
>>> In [ 30 ]:  x = np.array( [5 + 4j, 8 + 6j, 9 + 7j ] )
>>> In [ 31 ]:  x.dtype
>>> Out [ 31 ]:        dtype('complex128')
```
Bool
```
>>> In [ 32 ]:  y - np.array( [ False, True, False ] )
>>> In [ 33 ]:  y.dtype
>>> Out [ 33 ]:        dtype('bool')
```

Strings

>>> In [34]: z = np.array(['String1', 'String2', 'String3',])
>>> In [35]: f.dtype
>>> Out [35]:   dtype('S7')

We can convert one data type to another, which is also known as type casting. You are free to explicitly convert or cast the dtype of an array to any other ndarray's dtype by using the astype method.

Here is an example where integer values are getting casted to float values in the array.

In [36]:   x = np.array([10, 20, 30, 40, 50])

In [37]:   x.dtype
Out [37]:   dtype('int64')

In [38]:   float_y = x.astype(np.float64)

In [39]:   y.dtype
Out [39]:   dtype('float64')

If we cast float to integer, then the decimal part will be cut automatically as integer doesn't have the capacity to store the decimal part in it. Therefore, you need to remember that casting any float value to integer will truncate the decimal part automatically.

In [40]:   x = np.array([1.4, 2.5, 3.6, 4.8, 5.3, 6.7, 8.4, 9.6])

In[41]:   x
Out [41]:   array([1.4, 2.5, 3.6, 4.8, 5.3, 6.7, 8.4, 9.6])

In [42]:   x.astype(np.int32)

Out [42]:   array([1, 2, 3, 4, 5, 6, 7, 8, 9], dtype = int32)

If while doing type casting the attempts fail it will raise type error. There is a feature where another array's datatype can be used.

In [43]: array_int = np.arange(20)

In [44]: y = np.array([0.57, 0.38, 0.57, 0.86, 0.64, 0.45], dtype = np.float64)

In [45]: array_int.astype(y.dtype)

Out[45]: array([0., 1., 2., 3., 4., 5., 6., 7., 8., 9., 10., 11., 12., 13., 14., 15., 16., 17., 18., 19.])

Shortnotes: astype will create new array even if the new and old datatype are same. In complex data type keep in mind about floating point error as floating point datatypes can be used in certain points of decimal values.

Various Operations between Scalers and Arrays

The vectorization is defined as the process that gives you access for the batch operation on data without using for loops. When you perform any arithmetic operation between 2 similar size arrays, then that operation will be applied element wise among both the arrays.

You can see the below example for arithmetic operations (multiplication, addition, subtraction) between two arrays.

In [50]:   val
Out [50]:   val([[10, 20, 30] , [40, 50, 60]])

In [51]:   val * val
Out [51]:   array ([[100, 400, 900] , [1600, 2500, 3600]])

In [52]:   val - val
Out [52]:   array([[0, 0, 0] , [0, 0, 0]])

In [53]:   val + val
Out [53]:   array([[20, 40, 60] , [80, 100, 120]])

We can also do simple mathematical operation with arrays like division as well.

In [54]:   val / 2
Out [54]:   array([[5, 10,   15] , [20, 25, 30]])

Here are some arithmetic operations that can be applied on arrays.
>>> np.exp(a)   It is used for exponentiation
>>> np.sqrt(a) It is used to calculate the Square root
>>> np.sin(b)   It is used to print the sin values of the array elements
>>> np.cos(a)   It is used to print the cos values of the array elements
>>> np.log(b)   It is used to print the natural logarithm values of the array
                elements
>>> e.dot(c)   It is used to calculate the dot product of the two arrays

Basic Indexing and Slicing

In NumPy indexing and slicing of array is another important topic. In indexing, there are multiple ways of selecting array subset and in python indexing start with 0.

We can say that the 1-D arrays are quite simple in nature and they are similar to lists in Python.

In [55]:   x = np.arange(20)

In [56]:   x
Out [56]:   array([0, 1, 2, 3, 4, 5, 6, 7, 8, 9, 10, 11, 12, 13, 14, 15, 16, 17, 18, 19])

In [57]:   x[8]
Out [57]:   8

In [58]:   x[5 : 16]
Out [58]:   array([5, 6, 7, 8, 9, 10, 11, 12, 13, 14, 15])

In [59]:   x[5 : 9] = 6

In [60]:   x
Out [60]:   array([0, 1, 2, 3, 4, 6, 6, 6, 6, 9, 10, 11, 12, 13, 14, 15, 16, 17, 18, 19])

As you can see in the above example, when we assigned a particular scalar value to the array slice, i.e. x[5 : 9] = 6, the value got changed in the entire selection. Therefore, we can say that the array slices are the views of actual array. It implies that the data

111

doesn't get copied but instead the modified values will get reflected back in the original array.

In slicing the arrays are not modified, which means any changes will be reflected the original one. This technique will help in working with large amount of data where spaces are much more important things.

```
In [ 61 ]:    slice_arr = arr[5 : 8]
In [ 62 ]:    slice_arr[1] = 54321
In [ 63 ]:    x
Out [ 63 ]:   array( [ 0, 1, 2, 3, 4, 6, 54321, 6, 6, 9, 10, 11, 12, 13, 14, 15,
              16, 17, 18, 19 ] )
In [ 64 ]:    slice_arr[:] = 32
In [ 65 ]:    x
Out [ 65 ]:   array([ 0,  1,  2,  3,  4, 32, 32, 32,  8,  9, 10, 11, 12, 13, 14,
              15, 16, 17, 18, 19 ] )
```

You get many more options when you deal with high dimensional arrays. In high dimensional arrays the element in each index is one-dimensional array. That's why the elements can approached recursively. This can also be achieved by separating those by commas.

```
In [ 66 ]:    twoDarray = np.array( [ [ 10, 20, 30 ] , [ 40, 50, 60 ], [70,
              80, 90 ] ] )
In [ 67 ]:    twoDarray[1]
Out [ 67 ]:   array( [ 40, 50, 60 ] )
In [ 68 ]:    twoDarray[1][2]
Out [ 68 ]:   60
```

In [69]:   twoDarray[0, 1]
Out [69]:   20

In ndarrays, if later indices are omitted, the returned object will be a lower-dimensional ndarray, which includes higher dimensions' data.

In [70]:   threeDarray = np.array([[[10, 20, 30] , [40, 50, 60]] , [[70, 80, 90] , [100, 110, 120]]])
In [71]:   threeDarray
Out [71]:   array([[[10, 20, 30] , [40, 50, 60]] , [[70, 80, 90] , [100, 110, 120]]])
threeDarray[0] is an array of size 2 × 3
In [72]:   threeDarray[0]
Out [72]:   array([[10, 20, 30] , [40, 50, 60]])
We can assign arrays and scalar values to threeDarray[0]
In [73]:   last_values = threeDarray[0].copy()
In [74]:   threeDarray[0] = 21
In [75]:   threeDarray
Out [75]:   array([[[21, 21, 21] , [21, 21, 21]] , [[70, 80, 90] , [100, 110, 120]]])
In [76]:   threeDarray[0] = last_values
In [77]:   threeDarray
Out [77]:   array([[[10, 20, 30] , [40, 50, 60]] , [[70, 80, 90] , [100, 110, 120]]])

One thing to note above is that wherever we have selected the subsections of an array, views are returned back in the arrays.

Indexing with Slicing

The arrays can be sliced in the same syntax. Higher dimensional objects have more option of slicing. As you can see here, it can have many slices just like it has many indexes.

```
In [ 78 ]:      x[ 1:6 ]
Out [ 75 ]:     array( [ 1,  2,  3,  4, 32 ] )
```

If you mix integers slices and indexes, the lower dimensional slices will be achieved. A colon means to give the whole axis, so higher dimensional axes can be achieved using this.

Fancy Indexing

If the indexing is performed by integers array, then it is called fancy indexing.

```
In [ 76 ]:    x = np.empty( ( 8, 4 ) )
In [ 77 ]:    for j in range(8):  ......:    x[i] = i
In [ 78 ]:    x
Out [ 78 ]:   array( [ [ 10, 10, 10, 10 ] , [ 20, 20, 20, 20 ] , [ 30, 30, 30, 30 ]
              ,  [ 40, 40, 40, 40 ] ,  [ 50, 50, 50, 50 ] ,  [ 60, 60, 60, 60 ] ,
              [ 70, 70, 70, 70] ,   [ 80, 80, 80, 80 ] ] )
```

If you want to select particular rows or subsets of array you just have to pass a ndarray of data.

```
In [ 79 ]: x[ [5, 8, 1, 0 ] ]
Out [ 103 ]:
```

array([[5, 5, 5, 5] ,
    [8, 8, 8, 8] ,
    [0, 0, 0, 0] ,
    [1, 1, 1, 1]])

When we want to pass multiple ndarray then it takes a 1 dimensional array of elements corresponding to each indices:

In [80]:   x = np.arange(25).reshape((5, 5))
In [81]:   x
Out [81]:   array([[0, 1, 2, 3, 4] ,
                 [5, 6, 7, 8, 9] ,
                 [10, 11, 12, 13, 14] ,
               [15, 16, 17, 18, 19] ,
               [20, 21, 22, 23, 24]])
In [82]:   x[[0, 1, 2, 3, 4] , [0, 1, 2, 3, 4]]
Out [82]:   array([0, 6, 12, 18, 24])

In the above example, we selected the elements (0,0), (1,1), (2,2), (3,3), (4,4). Therefore, it showed the value present at those locations from the array.

Fancy indexing always copy the elements into array.

Universal Functions: Fast Element-wise Array Functions

The unfunc, or universal function, is defined as the function the perform operation on elements on ndarray element wise. It is a fast vectorized form that takes scaler and gives scaler products. There are many ufuncs available for you like sqrt, exp, etc.

Here are some examples:

In [83]: x = np.arange(20)

In [84]: np.sqrt(x)

Out [84]: array([0.00 , 1.00 , 1.4142, 1.7321, 2.00 , 2.2361, 2.4495, 2.6458, 2.8284, 3.00 , 3.162, 3.317, 3.464, 3.606, 3.742, 3.873, 4.00, 4.123, 4.243, 4.359])

The unary transformation functions are:

In [85]: a = randn(6)

In [86]: b = randn(6)

In [87]: a

Out [87]: array([0.7853, 0.2974, 0.5682, -0.5131, 0.6345, 0.6122])

In [88]: b

Out [88]: array([0.5687 , -0.3131, -0.74318, 0.8732, -1.1523, 0.8738])

In [89]: np.maximum(a, b) # It will give the maximum as per element wise

Out [89]: array([0.7853, 0.2974, 0.5682, 0.8732, 0.6345, 0.8738])

Now here is a list of universal functions.

Function Name	Description of the function
abs and fabs	It is uscd to calculate the element wise absolute value for float, integer, complex values, etc. We can use fabs instead of abs for faster calculations in data that is not complex.
sqrt	It is used to calculate the square root of every element present in the array.
square	It is used to calculate the square of every element present in the array.
exp	It is used to calculate the exponent ex of every element present in the array.
log, log2	It is used to calculate the natural logarithm (having base e) or (log base 2) of every element present in the array.
sign	It is used to provide the sign of every element present in the array (1, 0, -1).
ceil	It is used to calculate the ceiling of every element present in the array, i.e. the smallest integer that is >= to every element.

floor	It is used to calculate the floor every element present in the array, i.e. the smallest integer that is <= to every element.
rint	It is used to round off the array elements to the nearest integer and it doesn't change the dtype.
modf	It is used to return integer and fraction part of the array elements in a separate array.
isnan	It is used to return the boolean array, which indicates if every element present in the array is of NaN type or not. NaN means Not a Number.
Isfinite and isinf	It is used to return the boolean array, which indicates if every element present in the array is finite or infinite.
cos, sin, cosh	It is used to calculate the trigonometric functions for the array elements.
sinh, tanh, tan	It is used to calculate the trigonometric functions for the array elements.
arcsin, arccosh,arccos	It is used to calculate Inverse trigonometric functions.
logical_not	It is used to calculate the truth value of not x.

Here are some of the binary universal function.

Function name	Description of the function
add	It is used to add the corresponding elements of two different arrays
subtract	It is used to subtract corresponding elements preset in the second array from the first array
multiply	It is used to multiply the corresponding elements of two different arrays
divide	It is used to divide corresponding elements of two different arrays
power	It is used to raise the elements present in the first array to exponential powers mentioned in the second array
maximum	It is used to find out the maximum number from element wise array
minimum	It is used to find out the minimum number from element wise array
mod	It is used to find out the remainder after dividing two element wise arrays.
copysign	It is used to copy the sign of values present in the second argument into the values present in the first argument

Data Processing by using Arrays

The mathematical or statistical operation that requires loop to write in programming language, can be easily done using NumPy. This is defined as vectorization in programming domain. It works faster than python equivalent functions. So, in numerical computation the importance of this function is very important.

If we take an example, assume we want to evaluate a function that is the square root of an equation. The np.meshgrid takes one dimensional array as input and gives output 2 dimensional matrices.

In [90]: val = np.arange(-4, 4, 0.01)
In [91]: a, b = np.meshgrid(val, val)
In [92]: b
Out [92]: array([[-4. , -4. , -4. , ..., -4. , -4. , -4.] ,
            [-3.99, -3.99, ..., -3.99, -3.99, -3.99] ,
            [-3.98, -3.98, ..., -3.98, -3.98, -3.98] ,
            ...,
            [3.98, 3.98, ..., 3.98, 3.98, 3.98] ,
            [3.99, 3.99, ..., 3.99, 3.99, 3.99]])

Now the function will be evaluated in this way:
In [93]: import matplotlib.pyplot as plotting
In [94]: c = np.sqrt(a ** 2 + b ** 2)
In [95]: c
Out [95]: array([[6.071, 6.064, ..., 6.049, 6.056, 6.064] ,
            [6.064, 6.056, ..., 6.042, 6.049, 6.056] ,
            [6.0566, 6.049, ..., 6.0356, 6.042, 6.049] ,

...,
$$[\,6.049,\ 6.042,\ ...,\ 6.0286,\ 6.035,\ 6.042\,]\,,$$
$$[\,6.056,\ 6.049,\ ...,\ 6.035,\ 6.0428,\ 6.049\,]\,,$$
$$[\,6.064\,,\ 6.056,\ ...,\ 6.042,\ 6.0469,\ 6.056\,]\,]\,)$$

In [96]: plotting.imshow(c, cmap=plt.cm.gray); plt.colorbar()

Out [96]: <matplotlib.colorbar.Colorbar instance at 0x3e23d56>

In [97]: plotting.title(" Here is the plotting: $\sqrt {a^2 + b^2 } $ for values")

Out [97]: <matplotlib.text.Text at 0x2665794>

Here is how the output will look like for the above plotting:

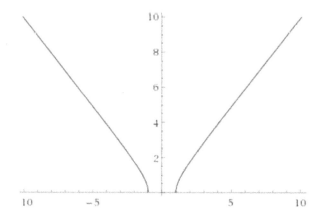

Expressing Conditional Logic

The np.where is supplementary expression of x if condition y operation. Assume some Boolean and normal array,

In [98]: arrayX = np.array([10, 11, 12, 13, 14])

In [99]: arrayY = np.array([20, 21, 22, 23, 24])

In [100]: boolCondition = np.array([True, False, True, True, False])

Also assume the wanted values are from xarr when the related value is true otherwise take value from yrrr. It can be written as,

In [101]: finalResult = [(a if c else b)   .....:

                for a, b, c in zip(arrayX, array, boolCondition)]

In [102]: finalResult

Out [102]: [10, 21, 12, 13, 24]

So, as we can see it is not fast and it is easily substituted by where function as this is a large array. Also it will not work with multi-dimensional arrays.

In [103]: finalResult = np.where(boolCondition, arrayX, arrayY)

In [104]: finalResult

Out [104]: array([10, 21, 12, 13, 25])

It is also used to create a ndarray based on another ndarray. For example, you have a matrix of random numbers and you would like to replace all the positive numbers in the matrix with 3 and all the negative numbers in the matrix by -3 respectively. Here is how you can do it using np.where very easily.

In [105]: x = randn(4, 4)

In [106]: x

Out [106]: array([[0.8372, 3.4313, 2.6934, 1.4653] ,

    [-2.5926, -2.1536, 1.4413, 1.3483] ,

        [-1.1798, 1.3299, 1.7827, -1.7585] ,

        [1.5857, 1.1619, 2.3583, 0.3865]])

In [107]: np.where(x > 0, 3, -3)

Out [107]: array([[3, 3, 3, 3] ,

        [-3, -3, 3, 3] ,

[-3, 3, 3, -3] ,
[3, 3, 3, -3]])
In [108]: np.where(x > 0, 3, x) # Here we are setting the positive values to 3
Out [108]: array([[3.   , 3.   , 3.   , 3.   ] ,
          [-2.5926, -2.1536, 3.   , 3.   ] ,
          [-1.1798, 3.   , 3.   , -1.7585] ,
          [3.   , 3.   , 3.   ,   0.3865]])

You can easily use the (where) clause to make your complicated logic easier to understand and implement. We can also convert for if elif condition in nested where function like following:

finalResult = []
for j in range(num):
        if condition1[j] and condition2[j]:
                finalResult.append(10)
        elif cond1[j]:
                finalResult.append(20)
        elif cond2[j]:
                finalResult.append(30)
        else:
                finalResult.append(40)
Now if we convert in nested where
np.where(condition1 & condition2, 0,
        np.where(condition1, 1,
                np.where(condition2, 2, 3)))

Here we this type of operation can be done in minutes using NumPy operators.

Mathematical and Statistical Methods

NumPy is used for basic mathematical as well as statistical operations also. Mean, standard deviation etc aggregation are done easily with this library by calling the top level function of NumPy or by using the array instance feature.

In [109]: x = np.random.randn(5, 4) # It will distribute the data normally
In [110]: x.mean()
Out [110]: 1.731646738673273748
In [111]: np.mean(x)
Out [111]: 1.731646738673273748
In [112]: x.sum()
Out [112]: 2.3632674167835627

Here is the list of methods that can be used in array statistics.

Function name	Description of the Function
sum	It is used to calculate the total of all the elements present in the array.
mean	It is used to calculate the arithmetic mean of all the elements present in the array.

std   It is used to calculate the standard deviation of elements present in the array.

var   It is used to calculate the variance of elements present in the array.

max   It is used to calculate the maximum from the elements present in the array.

Min   It is used to calculate the minimum from the elements present in the array.

cumsum   It is used to calculate the cumulative sum of all the elements present in the array starting from 0

cumprod   It is used to calculate the cumulative product of elements present in the array starting from 1

Sorting

NumPy can obviously do array sorting. With sort method, you can sort the elements of the array easily in ascending or descending order as per your requirement.

In [113]: x = randn(10)
In [114]: x
Out [114]: array([1.7903, 1.5678, 1.1968, -1.2349, 1.9979, 1.1185, -2.4147, -1.6425, 2.3476, 0.3243])
In [115]: arr.sort()

The np.sort method returns copy of the input array without changing the actual one. Therefore, you can sort the array first and then select the particular rank's value.

In [116]: sorted_arr = randn(1000)
In [117]: sorted_arr.sort()
In [118]: sorted_arr[int(0.02 * len (sorted_arr))]
Out [118]: -2.6802134371907113

Unique and Other Set Logic

NumPy has some very simple operations for 1D arrays. Such as unique, which is used in returning unique values from arrays.

In [119]: studentNames = np.array(['Mary', 'David', 'Mary', 'Mary', 'David', 'Mark', 'Mark'])
In [120]: np.unique(names)
Out [120]: array(['Mary', 'David', 'Mark'] , dtype='|S4')
In [121]: intValues = np.array([2, 2, 2, 1, 1, 0, 0, 3, 3])
In [122]: np.unique(intValues)
Out [122]: array([0, 1, 2, 3])

Here is the list of other set functions that can be used.

Function Name   **Description of the function**

unique(a)   It is used to compute the sorted and unique elements present in the array a

intersect1d(a, b) It is used to compute the sorted, common elements present in array a and b union1d(a, b)   It is used to compute the sorted union of elements in array a and b

in1d(a, b)   It is used to compute the boolean array, which indicates if every element of array a is present in array y or not

setxor1d(a, b)   It is used to set the symmetric differences between the arrays a and b i.e. elements that are present in only one of the arrays, but not in both.

File Input and Output with Arrays

NumPy can save and load data in txt or binary format. The np.save and np.load functions are used to load and save data in disk. The. npy extension is the file format in which array data are stored.

In [123]: x = np.arange(10)

In [124]: np.save(random_array', x)

In [125]: np.load('random_array.npy')

Out [125]: array([0, 1, 2, 3, 4, 5, 6, 7, 8, 9])

With np.savez you can save multiple file as zip extension.

In [126]: np.savez('array_archive.npz', a=x, b=x)

You can also work with txt file and csv file where data are comma separated. You can read and save the data as you want. Here is a comma separated file names arr_example:

In [127]: !cat arr_example.txt

1.246783, 2.346630, 0.060817, 2.336771, 1.395163, -1.133918, -
    1.536658, 1.236714

1.756410, 1.764607, -1.585624, 1.737556, -2.584313, 1.794476, -
    1.844203, 1.255487

0.572769, 2.730531, 2.532438, 0.836707, -1.477528, 2.425233,
    1.742803, 1.593734

In [128]: arr = np.loadtxt('arr_example.txt', delimiter = ',')

In [129]: arr

Out[129]: array ([[1.246783, 2.346630, 0.060817, 2.336771, 1.395163,
    -1.133918, -1.536658, 1.236714], [1.756410, 1.764607,
    -1.585624, 1.737556, -2.584313, 1.794476, -1.844203,
    1.255487],
    [0.572769, 2.730531, 2.532438, 0.836707, -1.477528,
    2.425233, 1.742803, 1.593734]])

The np.savetxt will do the reverse task that writing an array and save as txt file.

Random Number Generation

The np.random module is the supplement of a random function, which is a built in function in python for efficiently creating arrays with random sample values. We can get any high dimensional using standard normal distribution using normal function.

In [130]: data_sample = np.random.normal(size = (4, 4))

In [131]: data_sample

Out [131]: array([[1.2352, 1.4137, 1.6349, 1.3561],

[2.4549, -1.8246, -1.9423, -2.4813] ,
[-0.2347, -1.7519, 1.6712, -0.1540] ,
[1.2598, -0.6365, 1.5379, -1.7831]])

In [132]: from random import normalvariate

In [133]: X = 10000

In [134]: %timeit data_sample = [normalvariate(0, 1) for _ in xrange(X)] 1 loops, best of 2: 3.44 s per loop

In [135]: %timeit np.random.normal(size = X) 10 loops, best of 4: 68.5 ms per loop

Here is a list of partial functions present in numpy.random:

Function name	Description of the function
seed	It is used to seed data into the random number generator
rand	It is used to draw samples as per the given uniform distribution
randint	It is used to draw completely random integers as per the range of low to high
randn	It is used to draw samples from a normal distribution, which has the mean as 0 and the standard deviation is 1
shuffle	It is used to randomly shuffle a sequence in place

permutation	It is used to return a completely random permutation of a sequence or even a permuted range as well.
binomial	It is used to draw samples in a binomial distribution
normal	It is used to draw samples from a Gaussian distribution

Example: Random Walks

In the following application with diagram is a mathematical implementation of random walk through array operation. Let us assume, a simple random walk starting at zero and steps are 1 and -1, which happens with equal probability. The implementation of random walk with 1000 steps is as follows:

```
import random
initial_position = 0
total_walk = [initial_position]
total_steps = 1000
for j in xrange(total_steps):
        increment_step = 1 if random.randint(0, 1) else -1
        initial_position += increment_step
        total_walk.append(initial_position)
```

Below is the example plot for 100 values present in these random walks.

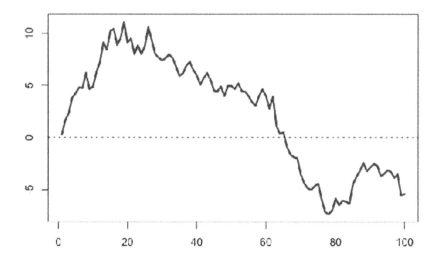

Here total walk can be defined as array expression and it is neither but the sum of random steps. So, we have to use this following function.

In [136]: steps = 1000
In [137]: totalDraws = np.random.randint(0, 2, size = steps)
In [138]: steps = np.where(totalDraws > 0, 1, -1)
In [139]: totalWalk = steps.cumsum()

The walk trajectory can be calculated from above. Apart from the walk trajectory, the minimum and maximum values also can be calculated. First crossing time will be a difficult statistical problem where the random steps to reach home will be calculated. We can calculate the time taken to reach or some steps far away from destination. The argmax function can be used, which gives us the max value of index in the terms of Boolean array.

In [140]: (np.abs(totalWalk) >= 10).argmax()
Out [140]: 39

The argmax function will not be proficient because it always reads the full array. Therefore, in this special scenario, as soon as we receive a True Boolean value, we take it as the maximum value.

Simulation of Many Random Walks at Once

If we change destination with 5000 steps, then with simple modification of previous code. The numpy.ran dom functions if passed a ndarray will create a 2D array of draws, and we can calculate the desirable sum across the rows to compute all 5,000 random walks.

In [141]: walks = 5000
In [142]: steps = 1000
In [143]: draws = np.random.randint(0, 2, size=(walks, steps)) # It will be either 1 or 0
In [144]: steps = np.where(draws > 0, 1, -1)
In [145]: walks = steps.cumsum(1)
In [146]: walks
Out [146] : array([[1, 0, 2, ..., 7, 6, 7],
                      [1, 0, -1, ..., 35, 34, 33],
                      [1, 0, -1, ..., 3, 4, 3],
                      ...,
                      [1, 2, 1, ..., 23, 24, 25],

132

$$[\ 1, \quad 2, \quad 3, ..., \quad 13, \ 12, \ 13 \ ] ,$$
$$[\ -1, \ -2, \ -3, ..., \ -23, \ -22, \ -21 \ ] \ ] \ )$$

The maximum and minimum values are

In [147]: walks.max()

Out [147]: 139

In [148]: walks.min()

Out [148]: -132

If the minimum crossing time varies from -35 to 35 then in 5000 walks those who reach are calculated in following way.

In [149]: hit35 = (np.abs(walks) >= 35).any(1)

In [150]: hit35

Out [150]: array([True, False, True, ..., True, False, True], dtype = bool)

In [151]: hit35.sum()

Out [151]: 3520

The Boolean array is used to get the walks that cross absolute 35 and argmax is called.

In [152]: cross_time = (np.abs(walks[hit35]) >= 35).argmax(1)

In [153]: cross_time.mean()

Out [153]: 487.35672535351

These are a few examples that give you some basic ideas about this library. Play with it solve many problems and try to code by yourself to clear your basics about it.

Chapter 5

Loading Data, File Formats and Storage

There is not much use of the tools listed in this book if you are unable to perform the data import and export using Python. We will stick to input/output methods related to pandas library only. Although there exist many other tools in various libraries for taking input and providing output such as NumPy.

The main purpose of using input & output in data analysis is to load the data from different databases, read csv text files as well as any other systematic disk format, and to interact with network web application programming interfaces (APIs).

How to Read and Write Data in Text Format

Python is considered a powerful programming language for manipulating text files because of its simple syntax to interact directly with the files, features such as tuple packing/unpacking, and well-built data structures.

There are numerous functions present in pandas library to perform read operation on tabular data. Here is a table listing some of the functions.

Function name	Description of the function
read_csv	It is used to load the data from a file or a URL using a delimiter. It uses comma as the default delimiter.
read_table	It is used to load the data from a file or a URL using a delimiter. It uses tab as the default delimiter.
read_fwf	It is used to read the data, which is present in a fixed width column format having no delimiters in it.
read_clipboard	It is a similar version of data_table. But it doesn't read the data from files and uses the clipboard data for reading purpose. Thus, it comes handy to convert tables present in webpages.

Let us see an overview about how to use the above functions for converting the text file's data into a DataFrame. Here are the options under which the above functions fall:

- Date-time parsing: It covers the combining power to combine date and time data present in numerous columns into one sole column while showing the result.
- Indexing: It has the capability to use one as well as more than one column while returning the DataFrame. It also has the option to choose or not to choose the column names present in the file.

- Iteration: It has the capability to support iteration of a large amount of data present in the large size files.
- Data conversion and type inference: It covers personalized list for the value markers, which are not present and conversions related to user defined values.
- Skipping data: It includes row, footer, and numeric data skipping from the file.

The most important feature for any function is type inference. By using it, we you don't need to worry about describing the column type like integer, string, boolean, numeric, etc. Let us see one example of csv file (comma separated values).

Let's see an example:
In [154]: !cat chapter05/csvExample1.csv
w, x, y, z, word
10, 20, 30, 40, this
50, 60, 70, 80, is
90, 100, 110, 120, fun

As it is a csv file, we can use the comma as a delimiter and use read_csv function to read the file into a DataFrame.
In [155]: df = pd.read_csv('chapter05/csvExample1.csv')
In [156]: df
Out [156]:

	w	x	y	z	word
0	10	20	30	40	this
1	50	60	70	80	is
2	90	100	110	120	fun

It can also be done using the read_table function by describing the delimiter.

In [157]: pd.read_table('chapter05/csvExample1.csv', sep=',')
Out [157]:

	w	x	y	z	word
0	10	20	30	40	this
1	50	60	70	80	is
2	90	100	110	120	fun

Note: We have used the cat shell command for printing the contents present in the file. If you are using Unix, and instead using Windows, you need to use the keyword "type" and not "cat" to print it on your screen.

It's not necessary that every file will have a header row. Let's see the below example:

In [158]: !cat chapter05/csvExample2.csv
10, 20, 30, 40, this
50, 60, 70, 80, is
90, 100, 110, 120, fun

We have two options to read this. One is to permit the pandas library to automatically assign the default column names. The other option is to specify the column names on your own.

In [159]: pd.read_csv('chapter05/csvExample2.csv', header = None)
Out [159]:

	X.1	X.2	X.3	X.4	X.5
0	10	20	30	40	this
1	50	60	70	80	is
2	90	100	110	120	fun

In [160]: pd.read_csv('chapter05/csvExample2.csv', names = ['w', 'x', 'y', 'z', 'word'])

Out [160]:

	w	x	y	z	word
0	10	20	30	40	this
1	50	60	70	80	is
2	90	100	110	120	fun

If you want to arrange the values in a hierarchy using multiple columns, you can pass the list of column names or numbers. Here is an example:

In [161]: !cat chapter05/csvExample3.csv
firstKey, secondKey, firstValue, secondValue
one, w, 10, 20
one, x, 30, 40
one, y, 50, 60
one, z, 70, 80
two, w, 90, 100
two, x, 110, 120
two, y, 130, 140
two, z, 150, 160

In [162]: parse_data = pd.read_csv(' chapter05/csvExample3.csv',
index_col=[' firstKey ', ' secondKey '])
In [163]: parse_data
Out [163]:

firstKey	secondKey	firstValue	secondValue
one	w	10	20
	x	30	40
	y	50	60
	z	70	80
two	w	90	100
	x	110	120
	y	130	140
	z	150	160

Parser function provides a lot of additional arguments, which can be used to handle many file format exceptions. For example, skiprows allows you to skip any rows present in the text file. Let's see an example:

In [164]: !cat chapter05/csvExample4.csv
Hi!
We are making it a little bit difficult for you
w, x, y, z, word
In today's modern world, you can easily skip any rows present in a file
10, 20, 30, 40, this
50, 60, 70, 80, is

90, 100, 110, 120, fun

In [165]: pd.read_csv(' chapter05/csvExample4.csv', skiprows = [0, 1, 3])

Out [165]:

	w	x	y	z	word
0	10	20	30	40	this
1	50		60	70	80	is
2	90	100	110	120	fun

A very important part in the parsing process, which is commonly used, is "Missing data handling". In these cases, either the missing data is not present in the file or it is marked as a sentinel value. In parsing, pandas use common sentinels like NA, NULL, and -1.

Now let us see an example:

In [166]: !cat chapter05/csvExample5.csv

anyValue , w, x, y, z, word

one, 10, 20, 30, 40, NA

NA, 50, 60 , , 80, is

three, NA, 100, 110, 120, fun

In [167]: final_result = pd.read_csv('chapter05/csvExample5.csv')

In [168]: final_result

Out [168]:

	anyValue	w	x	y	z	word
0	one	10	20	30	40	NaN
1	NaN	50	60	NaN	80	is
2	three	NaN	100	110	120	fun

In [169]: pd.isnull(final_result)

Out [169]:

	anyValue	w	x	y	z	word
0	False	False	False	False	False	True
1	True	False	False	True	False	False
2	False	True	False	False	False	False

The option na_values will either take a set of string values or a list while considering the missing values in the text file.

In [170]: final_result = pd.read_csv(' chapter05/csvExample5.csv', na_values = ['NULL'])

In [171]: final_result

Out [171]:

	anyValue	w	x	y	z	word
0	one	10	20	30	40	NaN
1	NaN	50	60	NaN	80	is
2	three	NaN	100	110	120	fun

We can specify fifferent NA sentinels for every column present in the text file.

Now let's see an example:

In [172]: sentinels = { 'word': ['fun', 'NA'], 'anyValue': ['one'] }

In [173]: pd.read_csv(chapter05/csvExample5.csv', na_values=sentinels)

Out [173]:

something a b c d message

	anyValue	w	x	y	z	word
0	NaN	10	20	30	40	NaN
1	NaN	50	60	NaN	80	is
2	three	NaN	100	110	120	NaN

Argument name	Description of the argument
Path	It is a string value that is used to indicate the location of file, file-like objects, or the URL.
Delimiter or sep	It is used to split the columns present in each row by either using a regular expression or a character sequence.
Names	It is used to show the result in form of column names, combined with the header value as None.
na_values	It is used to provide the sequence of values, which needs to be replaced by NA
Header	It is used to provide the row number that will be used as column names. The default value is 0 and is None in case there is no header row present in the file.
comment	It is used to split the character(s) comments after the end of lines.
date_parser	It is used for parsing dates from a text file.
index_col	It is used to provide the column names or numbers that need to be used as row index

	in result.
Nrows	It I used to pass the number of rows, which need to be read from the starting point of the file.
Verbose	It is used to print different output information, such as total number of missing values that are present in non-numeric columns.
Iterator	It is used to return the TextParser object to read the file in steps.
convertors	It is used to perform name mapping on functions.
skip_footer	It is used to provide the number of lines, which needs to be ignored at the end of the file.
Squeeze	It is used to return a series if the parsed data has only one column present in it.
chunksize	It is used to iterate and provide size of the file chunks.
encoding	It is used to provide the text encoding for Unicode system.
Dayfirst	It is used to deal with international format when ambiguous dates are getting parsed. Its default value is false.

How to Read Small Pieces of Text Files

In cases where we get huge files having lakhs of rows and columns in it, in order to process the file in the correct format, we need to read small chunks of file by iteration.

Now let us see an example:

In [174]: final_result = pd.read_csv('chapter05/example6.csv')

In [175]: final_result

Out [175]:

<class 'pandas.core.frame.DataFrame'>

Int64Index: 50000 entries, 0 to 49999

Data columns:

w 50000 non-null values

x 50000 non-null values

y 50000 non-null values

z 50000 non-null values

word 50000 non-null values

dtypes: int64(4), object(1)

We can see that this is a very large file having 50,000 rows in it. Therefore, we will read the file in small pieces of rows instead of reading the complete file. It can be done using "nrows".

In [176]: pd.read_csv('chapter05/example6.csv', nrows = 10)

Out [176]:

	w	x	y	z	word
0	10	20	30	40	A
1	50	60	70	80	B

2	90	100	110	120	C
3	130	140	150	160	D
4	170	180	190	200	E
5	10	20	30	40	F
6	50	60	70	80	G
7	90	100	110	120	H
8	130	140	150	160	I
9	170	180	190	200	J

In order to read the file, we can also use chunksize for number of rows.

In [177]: file_chunker = pd.read_csv('chapter05/example6.csv', chunksize = 500)

In [178]: file_chunker

Out [178]: <pandas.io.parsers.TextParser at 0x8398150>

TextParser object gets returned from read_csv will be iterating the file as per the chunksize fixed above i.e. 500. Therefore, we can aggregate the total value counts in "key" column by iterating the example6 file.

```
file_chunker = pd.read_csv('chapter05/example6.csv', chunksize = 500)
total = Series( [] )
for data_piece in file_chunker:
total = total.add( data_piece[ 'key' ].value_counts(), fill_value = 0 )
total = total.order(ascending = False)
```

Now we will get the below result:

In [179]: total[:10]

Out [179]:

F 460

Y 452

J 445

P 438

R 429

N 417

K 407

V 400

B 391

D 387

TextParser also has a get_chunk method. It helps us to read the pieces of random size from the file.

How to Write Data Out to Text Format?

We can export data in a delimited format as well by reading it from the csv file. Now let us see an example:

In [180]: final_data = pd.read_csv('chapter05/example5.csv')
In [181]: final_data
Out [181]:

	anyValue	w	x	y	z	word
0	one	10	20	30	40	NaN
1	two	50	60	NaN	80	is
2	three	NaN	100	110	120	fun

Now by using the to_csv method found in DataFrame, we can write the resultant data in a comma separated file easily.

In [182]: final_data.to_csv('chapter05/csv_out.csv')

In [183]: !cat chapter05/csv_out.csv

, anyValue, w, x, y, z, word

0, one, 10, 20, 30, 40,

1, two, 50, 60, , 80, is

2, three, 90, 100, 110, 120, fun

You are free to use any other delimiter as well and is not limited to comma only.

In [184]: final_data.to_csv(sys.stdout, sep = '|')

| anyValue| w| x| y| z| word

0| one| 10| 20| 30| 40|

1| two| 50| 60| | 80| is

2| three| 90| 100| 110| 120| fun

All the missing values will show up as empty in the output. You can replace them with any sentinel of your choice.

In [185]: final_data.to_csv(sys.stdout, na_rep = 'NA')

, anyValue, w, x, y, z, word

0, one, 10, 20, 30, 40, NA

1, two, 50, 60, NA, 80, is

2, three, 90, 100, 110, 120, fun

Reading Delimited Formats Manually

By using functions like read_table, we are able to load almost 90% tabular data from the disk. But, in some cases, manual intervention may be required to process the data. We might receive a file that has one or multiple malformed lines that fail the read_table function while loading the data. Now let us see an example:

In [186]: !cat chapter05/example7.csv
"x", "y", "z"
"10", "20", "30", "40"
"10", "20", "30", "40", "50"

We can use Python' built in csv module on order to read a file having only 1-character delimiter in it.

To do so, we need to pass the file to the csv.reader function.
import csv
foo = open('chapter05/example7.csv')
obj_reader = csv.reader(foo)

When we will iterate obj_reader as a field, it will provide the result by removing the quote characters automatically.

In [187]: for line in obj_reader:
.....: print line
['x', 'y', 'z']
['10', '20', '30', '40']
['10', '20', '30', '40', '50']

Now from here, it is your decision to perform wrangling in order to manipulate the data in your own form. Now let us see an example:

In [188]: output_lines = list(csv.reader(open('chapter05/example7.csv')))
In [189]: header, values = output_lines[0], output_lines[1:]
In [190]: obj_dict = { i: v for i, v in zip(header, zip(*values)) }
In [191]: obj_dict
Out [191]: {'x': ('10', '10'), 'y': ('20', '20'), 'z': ('30', '30') }

Comma separated values i.e. cs files have various formats. You can define your own new format having a specific delimiter, line terminator. You simply need to define a subclass of csv.Dialect to achieve this. Here is an example:

```
class own_dialect(csv.Dialect):
line_terminator = '\n'
value_delimiter = ';'
quote_char = ""
obj_reader = csv.reader(foo, dialect = own_dialect)
```

You can also use dialect parameters directly as keywords and no need to define a subclass.

```
obj_reader = csv.reader(foo, delimiter = '|')
```

In order to manually write the delimited files, we can use the csv.writer function. It will accept the same file and dialect options as the csv.reader function. Let's see an example.

```
with open('delimited_data.csv', 'w') as foo:
obj_writer = csv.writer(foo, dialect = own_dialect)
obj_writer.writerow( (x, 'y', 'z') )
obj_writer.writerow( ('10', '20', '30') )
obj_writer.writerow( ('40', '50', '60') )
```

Data in Binary Format

The best way to store data safely in the binary format is to use Python's built-in pickle serialization. For your convenience, all objects in pandas provide a save function to write the data as a pickle.

Now let us see an example:
```
In [ 192 ]: obj_frame = pd.read_csv('chapter05/example1.csv')
In [ 193 ]: obj_frame
Out [ 193 ]:
w, x, y, z, word
10, 20, 30, 40, this
50, 60, 70, 80, is
90, 100, 110, 120, fun
In [ 194 ]: obj_frame.save('chapter05/pickle_frame')
```

We can read back the data into Python using the pandas.load function.

In [195]: pd.load('chapter05/pickle_frame')

Out [195]:

w, x, y, z, word

10, 20, 30, 40, this

50, 60, 70, 80, is

90, 100, 110, 120, fun

Note: You can use pickle only for a short term storage format because it is not 100% guaranteed that the pickle format will be formed and solid with time. A newer version of the library might not unpickle an object that has been pickled today.

HDF5 Format

Various tools are present in order to read and write a large amount of data efficiently in binary format. One such widely used library is HDF5, which has an interface for many programming languages, such as Python, MATLAB, and Java. Full form of HDF is hierarchical data format. Every HDF5 has a file system like node structure. It helps you in storing more than one datasets as well as supports metadata (data about data). As compared to simple formats, it supports fast compression, which in turn helps in storing repeated pattern data efficiently. HDF5 is an excellent choice for reading and writing large datasets that do not fit in the memory, as it will cover tiny sections of huge arrays.

HDF5 library has 2 interfaces in Python: h5py and PyTables. Both of them follow a different approach to resolve a problem. PyTables abstracts the details of HDF5 in order to come up with querying ability, efficient data containers, and table indexing. Whereas h5py offers a simple and direct high level interface for the HDF5 API.

For storing pandas object, HDFStore class is used. Let's see it in the below example.

```
In [ 196 ]: obj_store = pd.HDFStore(owndata.h5')
In [ 197 ]: obj_store['obj1'] = obj_frame
In [ 198 ]: obj_store['obj1_col'] = obj_frame['a']
In [ 199 ]: obj_store
Out [ 199 ]:
<class 'pandas.io.pytables.HDFStore'>
File path: owndata.h5
obj1 DataFrame
obj1_col Series
Objects present in the HDF5 file are retireived back in a dict style.
In [ 200 ]: obj_store['obj1']
Out [ 200 ]:
w, x, y, z, word
10, 20, 30, 40, this
50, 60, 70, 80, is
90, 100, 110, 120, fun
```

Therefore, if you usually work with huge data files, you can explore more about h5py and PyTables as per your needs and requirements.

As most of the data analysis approaches are IO- bound and not CPU-bound, using HDF5 will speed up your application.

Reading MS Excel Files

You can use the ExcelFile class of pandas to read tabular data present in Microsoft Excel 2003 and higher versions. There are 2 packages present in the ExcelFile class: openpyxl and xlrd. Therefore, the first step is to install them.

In order to use the ExcelFile class, you need to create an instance of the class by passing the xls or xlsx file path as an argument.

File_xls = pd.ExcelFile('mydata.xls')

Now you can read the data that is present in the sheet using parse.

Data stored in a sheet can then be read into DataFrame using parse:

obj_table = File_xls.parse('Sheet')

Dealing with HTML and Web APIs

A rage number of websites offers public APIs (Application programming interface) in order to provide data feeds in JSON format or any other format as well. We have many ways to access those APIs using Python. One of the easiest methods is to use the request package using the link *http://docs.python-requests.org.*

If you want to search the words "pandas library" on Twitter website, you can use the HTTP GET request to do so.

Now let us see an example:

```
In [ 201 ]: import requests
In [ 202 ]: obj_url =
'https://search.twitter.com/search.json?q=pandas%20library'
In [ 203 ]: obj_resp = requests.get(obj_url)
In [ 204 ]: obj_resp
Out [ 204 ]: <Response [200]>
```

The text attribute of Response object has the content details returned by the GET query. Most of the web APIs returns a string in JSON format, which need to be loaded in a Python object.

```
In [ 205 ]: import json
In [ 206 ]: obj_data = json.loads(obj_resp.text)
In [ 207 ]: obj_data.keys()
Out [ 207 ]:
[u'next_page',
u'max_id_str',
u'completed_in',
u'refresh_url',
u'since_id_str',
u'since_id',
u'results',
u'query',
u'results_per_page',
```

u'page',

u'max_id']

In the above response, "results" field has the details of list of tweets, which look like the one below.

{u'created_at': u'Tue, 24 Jul 2019 09:35:41 +0000',

u'from_user': u'Mary',

u'from_user_id': 252475752,

u'from_user_id_str': u'252475752',

u'from_user_name': u'Mary Soloman',

u'geo': None,

u'id': 872586217459463892,

u'id_str': u'872586217459463892',

u'iso_language_code': u'pt',

u'metadata': {u'result_type': u'recent'},

u'source': u'<a href="https://twitter.com/">web</a>',

u'text': u'Lunchtime pandas-fu http://t.co/SI70xZZQ #pydata',

u'to_user': None,

u'to_user_id': 0,

u'to_user_id_str': u'0',

u'to_user_name': None}

Now you can use the fields that you want to pass to the DataFrame for further processing as per your needs and requirements.

Interaction with other Databases

Most of the applications do not use simple text files for storing the data as it is not a recommended method to a store huge amount of data. Mostly, relational databases are used to store the data like MYSQL, PostgreSQL, and SQL Server. NoSQL has also become very popular now a day and is also used widely. While choosing the correct database for the application, many points are taken into consideration like the below ones:

- Performance of the application
- Scalability needs and requirements
- Data integrity
- Data safety
- Easiness to handle the data

Loading the SQL Data into a Python DataFrame is a very simple and straightforward process. To make it much simpler, pandas library has some functions in this regard. Let's see an example of SQLite database utilizing sqlite3 driver present in Python.

Now let us see an example:

```
import sqlite3
myquery = """
CREATE TABLE example
(w VARCHAR(10), x VARCHAR(10),
y REAL, z INTEGER) ;"""
obj_con = sqlite3.connect(':memory:')
obj_con.execute(myquery)
```

obj_con.commit()

Now we will insert some data in the database.

obj_data = [('Mary', 'USA', 2.5, 26),

('John', 'Canada', 3.5, 30),

('David', 'UK', 3.8, 32),

('Alex', 'Germany', 4.6, 24)]

obj_stmt = "INSERT INTO example VALUES(?, ?, ?, ?)"

obj_con.executemany(obj_stmt, obj_data)

obj_con.commit()

When selecting the data from a table, SQL Drivers in Python (such as MySQLdb, PyODBC, pymssql, psycopg2, etc.) will return the list of tuples.

In [208]: obj_cursor = obj_con.execute('select * from example')

In [209]: obj_rows = obj_cursor.fetchall()

In [210]: obj_rows

Out [210]:

[(u'Mary', 'USA', 2.5, 26),

(u'John', 'Canada', 3.5, 30),

(u'David', 'UK', 3.8, 32),

(u'Alex', 'Germany', 4.6, 24)]

Now we can pass this list directly to the DataFrame's constructor along with the column names present in the description attribute of the cursor.

Now let us see an example:

In [211]: obj_cursor.description

Out [211]:

(('w', None, None, None, None, None, None),

('x', None, None, None, None, None, None),

('y', None, None, None, None, None, None),

('z', None, None, None, None, None, None))

In [212]: DataFrame(rows,

columns=zip(*obj_cursor.description)[0])

Out [212]:

	w	x	y	z
0	Mary	USA	2.5	26
1	John	Canada	3.5	30
2	David	UK	3.8	32
3	Alex	Germany	4.6	24

It is like munging so that you won't need to repeat it every time when you are querying the database. There is a read_frame function in pandas, which simplifies the entire process. You only need to pass the select query statement and the connection object created by you.

In [213]: import pandas.io.sql as obj_sql

In [213]: obj_sql.read_frame('select * from example', obj_con)

Out [213]:

	w	x	y	z
0	Mary	USA	2.5	26
1	John	Canada	3.5	30
2	David	UK	3.8	32
3	Alex	Germany	4.6	24

Store and Load Data in the MongoDB Database

There are many different forms of NoSQL database. Some of them are document based, while others are like the dict key-value pairs. We are using MongoDB as an example. Firstly, we need to start the MongoDB instance in our local machine. Then we will connect it to the default post by using the pymongo driver. Let's see the below example:

```
import pymongo
obj_con = pymongo.Connection('localhost', port = 8888)
```

The documents that are present in MongoDB can be found in the database collections. When we start the instance of MongoDB server, it can connect to multiple databases, and every database has multiple collections. Let's say, for example, we want to store API data from Twitter, which we have used in the chapter earlier. The very first step is to access a collection of tweets that should currently having no values in it.

Now let us see an example:

```
obj_tweets = obj_con.db.tweets
```

Now, we will load the tweets list. Then write the entire list to the collection by the help of tweets.save function:

```
import requests, json
obj_url ⁻
'http://search.twitter.com/search.json?q=python%20library'
obj_data = json.loads(requests.get(obj_url).text)
for obj_tweet in obj_data['results']:
```

obj_tweets.save(tweet)

Thus, we can easily have a list of all the tweets posted on Twitter using the collection. It can be done using the below syntax.

obj_cursor = obj_tweets.find({'from_user': 'Mary'})

An iterator will be returned back by the cursor, which yield all the documents as a dict. Thus, we can easily convert it into a Python DataFrame and extract the subset of all the fields of the tweet.
all_fields = ['from_user', 'created_at', 'text', 'id']
obj_value = DataFrame(list(obj_cursor), columns = all_fields)

Chapter 6

Plotting Data and Visualization in Python

Data analysis is all about presenting the information in a creative and interactive way. It is undoubtedly the most significant and essential process in data analysis. It is mostly used to get details regarding pre experimentation or post experimentation results using data plots. It helps in identifying the outliers, coming up with exciting ideas to transform business, and for data transformations. Python offers numerous data visualization tools, but we will focus on matplotlib. It can be found at http://matplotlib.sourceforge.net

Matplotlib is a 2-Dimensional plotting package, which come on the desktop. It was created in 2002 by John Hunter so that we can use MATLAB type of quality plots in Python. Today, matplotlib is fully compatible with Python to provide a productive and functional environment for computing services. It offers high end features such as panning and zooming when we use it in Graphical User Interface toolkit such as IPython. It offers support for numerous GUI backend applications and is independent of the Operating system. In addition to that, it has the capability to export the graphics into the raster formats such as PDF, JPG, GIF, SVG, BMP, PNG, etc.

It also offers various add-on toolkits for creating 3 Dimensional plots, projections, and mapping the relevant data. Some of the add-on toolkits are basemap and mplot3d. We will see how basemap is used to plot data into a map in this chapter. In order to understand the examples used in this chapter, you need to start IPython in Pylab mode. You can do this by using the pylab command. Otherwise, you can also enable the GUI event loop integration. You can do this by using the %gui command.

Matplotlib API Primer

We can interact with matplotlib in numerous ways. The very basic methd is to use pylab mode. It will automatically change the configuration of IPython to support the backend GUI of your preferred choice. You can use from a variety of options such as PyQt, Tk, GTK, wxPython, and Mac OS X native. You can also continue with the default GUI backend if you don't want to use our own. While using the Pylab mode, it will automatically import all the required functions and modules in IPython library so that you get a similar look and feel of MATLAB. To check if everything has been set up correctly, you can create a simple plot and check it. You can do it by using the arange magic command.

Plot(np.arange(20))

A new pop up window will open up with a simple line plot on your screen if the configuration is set up correctly. You can check it and then close it by entering close() or using your mouse/touchpad.

Functions such as plot and close present in matplotlib can be easily imported using the below syntax:

import matplotlib.pyplot as obj_plt

Using Subplots and Figures

The figure object contains the plots in the matplotlib library. With the help of obj_plt.figure function, we can easily create new figures.

In [1]: obj_fig = obj_plt.figure()

An empty pop-up window will appear when you are in the pylab mode. Figure function offers numerous options to choose from, with the most important being figsize, which helps to ensure that the created figure has a definite size as well as aspect ratio when saved to a disk. It also supports the numbering scheme, which looks similar to MATLAB. We can get the active figure's reference using the obj_plt.gcf function.

One thing to note here is that it is not possible to create a plot having an empty figure. There should be at least one subplot already present. We can create it using the add_subplot function.

In [2]: axis1 = obj_fig.add_subplot(3, 3, 1)

It means that a figure will be created that will have the dimensions 3 x 3 and we will be selecting initial 9 subplots that are numbered from 1.

If you create the next two subplots, you'll end up with a figure that looks like Figure 8-2.

In [3]: axis2 = obj_fig.add_subplot(3, 3, 2)
In [4]: axis3 = obj_fig.add_subplot(3, 3, 3)

For example, let's give a command to plot like this one: obj_plt.plot([4, 2.5, -3, 2.3]).

Now the matplotlib will draw on the last figure.

In [5]: from numpy.random import obj_rand
In [6]: obj_plt.plot(obj_rand(30).cumsum(), 'k--')

Here the k—refers to a styling option that commands matplotlib for plotting a black dash line. The Axes Subplot objects that are returned by obj_fig.add_subplot function can be plotted directly on other subplots that are empty. This is done by calling their instance methods.

In [7]: _ = axis1.hist(obj_rand(50), bins = 10, color = 'k', alpha = 0.25)
In [8]: axis2.scatter(np.arange(15), np.arange(15) + 3 * obj_rand(30))

You can check the matplotlib official documentation to know more about the advance features of plot types.

The most frequently used task is to create a figure having more than one subplots in it. To make this simple for the users, matplotlib has a function named obj_plt.subplots(). This function is used to create a new figure and then return the subplot objects in a NumPy array.

Now let us see an example:

In [9]: obj_fig, obj_axes = obj_plt.subplots(2, 3)

In [10]: obj_axes

Out [10]:

array([[Axes(0.245, 0.347257 ; 0.152684 x 0.415783),

Axes(0.452525, 0.347257 ; 0.152684 x 0.415783),

Axes(0.252059, 0.347257 ; 0.152684x 0.415783)],

[Axes(0.245, 0.2 ; 0.152684 x 0.415783),

Axes(0.452525, 0.2 ; 0.152684 x 0.415783),

Axes(0.252059, 0.2 ; 0.152684 x 0.415783)]], dtype = object)

It comes out to be very handy as the axes array works like 2-D array. We can also point out the subplots that are having similar X or Y axis by the help of sharex & sharey. This proves to be important when we want to compare the data on a similar scale, or else it will auto scale the limits on its own.

Here is the list of options available with the subplots function.

Argument name	Description of the argument
Nrows	It is used to return the number of rows present in the subplots
Ncols	It is used to return the number of columns present in the subplots
Sharex	It is used to make sure that all the subplots are using same X axis ticks
Sharey	It is used to make sure that all the subplots are using same Y axis ticks

subplot_kw	It is used to provide the dict of all the keywords to create the subplots

Balancing the Spaces near Subplots

Matplotlib library allows some empty space around the subplots by default. This is in proportion to the length and breadth of the plot. Therefore, if we will increase or decrease the size of the plot, then the spacing will also get resized dynamically. You can increase or decrease the plot size by manually adjusting the Graphical User Interface window or by writing the program. The subplots_adjust function allows us to easily change the spacing from all directions like Top, Bottom, Left or Right.

You can see the below example:

subplots_adjust(bottom=None, top=None, left=None, right=None, hspace=None, wspace=None)

Here hspace controls the height of the figure whereas wspace is used to control the width. Here is an example:

```
obj_fig, obj_axes = obj_plt.subplots(3, 3, sharex = True, sharey = True)
for x in range(3):
for y in range(3):
obj_axes[x, y].hist(obj_rand(100), bins = 10, color = 'k', alpha = 0.2)
obj_plt.subplots_adjust(wspace = 0, hspace = 0)
```

Note: The axis labels might overlap with each other. This is because matplotlib will not check if the labels are getting overlapped or not. For this, we need to use the tick labels and locations on our own.

Markers, Colors, and Line Styles

The X and Y co-ordinates of the main plot function will accept optional arguments for the line style and color coding. We can plot the data with any color we want.

Here is an example:
ax.plot(x, y, 'b ')
Another example to plot it using the desired color and style is:
ax.plot(x, y, color = 'b', linestyle = '--')

It offers numerous colors and it can be created by using the RGB (Red, Green, Blue) values.

We can also use markers for highlighting the important data points. As we know that matplotlib will be creating a continuous plot line, it becomes difficult to find out where the exact point lies. To overcome this problem, markers are used.

In [10]: obj_plt.plot(obj_rand(20).cumsum(), 'ko--')

Labels and Ticks

We have two options to customize the plots. The first option is to use the pyplot interface, which is similar to the MATLAB. The second option is to use the matplotlib API for object oriented design.

Functions like xticks and xlim are present in pyplot interface and make it intuitive and useful for decorating plots. They have the capability to control the tick locations ad labels. Here is how you can use them:

- When we call the function without any arguments, it will return the value of the current parameter only. Therefore, only the plotting range is returned.
- When we call the function with the arguments, it will set the parameter values automatically. Therefore, it will set the range from 0 to 20 if we give the arguments as 0, 20.

All these functions will work on the most recent AxesSubplot i.e. the newest one that has been created. They will be corresponding to 2 functions on the subplot and they are: get_xlim() and set_xlim().

We can create a simple random walk plot to understand how the axis customization works.

In [11]: obj_fig = obj_plt.figure();
      obj_ax = obj_fig.add_subplot(2, 2, 2)
In [12]: obj_ax.plot(obj_rand(500).cumsum())

In order to change the ticks on X axis, we can use the set_xticks combined with set_xticklabels functions. Set_xticks function will command the matplotlib library to place tick points on the data range. Set_xticklabels will allow you to set any value as labels.

In [13]: obj_ticks = obj_ax.set_xticks([5, 80, 150, 320, 500])

In [14]: obj_labels = obj_ax.set_xticklabels(['Number1', 'Number2', 'Number3', 'Number4', 'Number5'],

   ....:   rotation = 20, fontsize = 'small')

Finally, we can use the set_xlable function to provide a name to the X axis and also set the title using set_title function.

In [15]: obj_ax.set_title(' This is the first plot created by me in matplotlib')

Out[15]: <matplotlib.text.Text at 0x5f8290912851>

In [16]: obj_ax.set_xlabel(' Various Stages')

Saving the Plots

We can easily save the active plots in a file using the savefig function. This function is the same as the savefig function of the Figure object. In order to save SVG type of a figure, we need to give the below command:

obj_savefig('Example1.svg')

In this case, file type gets inferred directly from the file's extension itself. Therefore, if we will use a .PDF version instead, we will automatically get a PDF file saved in the location. Most of us use some of the common controls in a graphic object i.e. dpi and bbox inches.

DPI is known as dots per inch resolution. BBox_inches has the ability to trim all the surrounding whitespaces present around the original figure. In order to get the exact plot above by using the minimal whitespace area around the plot, we can use the below command:

obj_savefig('Example1.png', dpi = 300, bbox_inches = 'tight')

Not only savefig function writes the plot to a disk, but it can also write it to any similar object like StringIO. It turns out to be very helpful while serving the dynamic images over the web that are generated by a query.

We can also use many arguments in the savefig function like the below ones.

1. Fname: It is used to provide the path of the file in a string format or a file like object's location. The format of the figure gets inferred automatically using the file's extension such as png, pdf, etc.

2. Format: It is used to provide the file format that needs to be used explicitly in case you don't want it to get picked automatically from the file extension. Supported file formats are pdf, png, ps, eps, svg, etc.

3. Dpi: It is used to provide the resolution for the figure in dots per inch. It uses a default value of 100 and can be configured to any other value as well.

4. Facecolor: It is used to configure the background color of the figure that is outside the subplots. It uses a default value of white, which is dented by (w).

5. Bbox_inches: It is used to specify the exact portion of the figure that we need to save. We can pass "tight" value in it, which will in turn automatically trim all the empty whitespaces around the entire figure.

Configuring Matplotlib Library

Various color schemes are preloaded in matplotlib so that figures are created beautifully and looks appealing to the end user. There are many parameters that help in customizing the default figure. They include colors, style of grids, figure size, size of font, spacing options etc. We have two methods in order to configure the matplotlib system. The first method is to do it via programmatically using the rc() function present in Python. Let's say, we want to set the global size for default figure to be 12 x 14. We can use the below command:

obj_plt.rc('figure', figsize = (12, 14))

In the above example, the first command passed to the rc function is the component that we would like to customize. It can have values like axes, figure, ytick, xtick, legend, grid, etc. Once we have passed that, the next argument to be passed is the parameters value, which you want to set on the component.

If you need to know more details about advanced customization of files and objects, there is a matplotlibrc configuration file present in the matplotlib directory.

Function Plotting in Pandas

Till now we have seen matplotlib and by now you must have understood that it is a low level tool. We can create a plot using the very basic components and then display the data using features like line, box, bar, contour, scatter, tick labels, title, etc. This is required because the required data, which is necessary for completing the entire plot, is spread out in more than one object.

Whereas in pandas, it is not the case. We have the row label values, column label values, and all the required possible group information with us already. It implies that fully customizable plots, which require a lot of code to create, are easily accessible in pandas by using a couple of lines of code. Thus, pandas offer high level plotting functions in order to create appealing visualizations and we get well organized data in the DataFrame objects.

Plotting Lines

Both DataFrame and Series offers a plotting method of their own in order to create various type of plots. The default type of plot for both of them is the line plot. We can create it using the below example:

In [14]: plot_series = Series(np.random.randn(15).cumsum(), index = np.arange(0, 50, 5))

In [15]: plot_series.plot()

Here we are passing the index of series object to the matplotlib to plot the values on the X axis. We can disable it as well by passing the argument use_index = False. There are 2 options for adjusting the X axis and Y axis ticks and limits. They are: xticks and xlim.

Here is a simple series plot indicating the X axis and Y axis plotting.

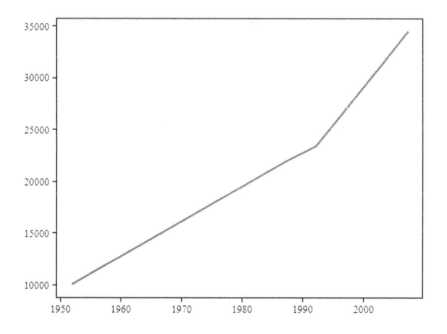

Almost all the plotting functions present in pandas will accept the optional parameter ax as the subplot object. It provides much needed flexibility in placing the subplots in gird layout.

Plot method present in DataFrame will plot every column present in it at a different line in the same subplot. Thus, a legend gets created automatically. Here is an example of the same.

In [16]: plot_df = DataFrame(np.random.randn(20, 5).cumsum(0),

    ....: columns = ['W', 'X', 'Y', 'Z'],

    ....: index = np.arange(0, 50, 50))

In [17]: plot_df.plot()

Here is a simple DataFrame plot indicating the X axis and Y axis plotting.

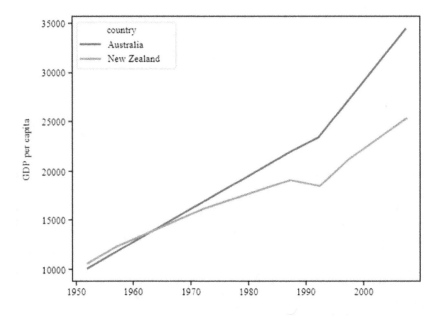

Let us see the arguments that can be used in the plot method of Series.

1. Label: It is used to provide the label value in order to plot the legend.

2. Style: It is used to pass the style of the line of plotting. For example, we can pass ko—value to matplotlib.

3. Logy: It is used to provide log scaling values on the Y axis.

4. Rot: It is used to rotate the tick labels from 0 to 360 degrees.

5. Kind: It is used to provide the component type. It can have values like bar, line, kde, barh.

6. Xticks: It is used to pass the values used for ticks on X axis.

7. Yticks: It is used to pass the values used for ticks on Y axis.

8. Use_index: It is used to provide index value of the object to be used for tick labels.

9. Xlim: It is used to set the limits on X axis. For example, we can use [(0, 20)]

10. Ylim: It is used to set the limits on X axis. For example, we can use [(0, 10)]

11. Alpha: It is used to pass the opacity for the plot filling. It can range from zero to one.

DataFrame can handle columns pretty well by the help of various flexible options. It can plot all the columns on a same subplot or more than one as well.

Plotting Bars

We can easily create bar plots by passing the value kind = 'bar' in case of vertical bars. If you want to use horizontal bars, then you need to use kind = 'barh'. Here is an example of the same:

In [17]: obj_fig, obj_axes = obj_plt.subplots(2, 1)
In [18]: obj_data = Series(np.random.rand(12), index = list('a b c d e f g h I j k l'))
In [19]: obj_data.plot(kind = 'bar', ax = axes[0], color = 'k', alpha = 0.4)
Out [19]: <matplotlib.axes.AxesSubplot at 0x3de6851>
In [20]: obj_data.plot(kind = 'barh', ax = axes[1], color = 'k', alpha = 0.4)

We can also create stacked bar plots using DataFrame. For that, we need to pass the argument value stacked = True. This will stack together all the values in every row.

In [32]: obj_df.plot(kind = 'barh', stacked = True, alpha = 0.4)

Scatter Plots

It is very important to use scatter plots in order to examine the relationship between 2 data series of 1-Dimensional values. Here, each point's co-ordinates are specified using to different DataFrame columns. These are filled circles that represent those points. The points can be anything from a pair of metrics to longitude & latitude values in a map.

Now let us see how we can draw a scatter plot by using the co-ordinate values present in the columns of DataFrame.

```
>>> obj_df = pd.DataFrame( [ [2.5, 1.5, 1], [3.7, 2.03 0], [6.5, 3.6, 1],
...            [4.4, 1.2, 1], [6.3, 2.0, 1] ],
...            columns = [ 'length', 'width', 'species' ] )
>>> axis1 = obj_df.plot.scatter( x = 'length',
...            y = 'width',
...            c = 'DarkBlue')
```

After executing the above code, we will get the plot as shown in the below image.

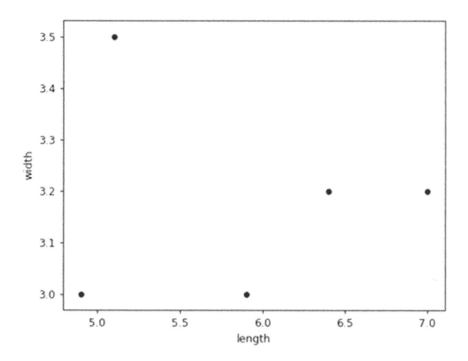

In the above example, we have passed parameter values of x, y, s (scalar or array), and c (color).

Conclusion

Python Tools

Since it is an open source, there are numerous options to create data visualizations in Python. We can choose from the free ones to the commercial paid libraries with Python. We mainly discussed matplotlib with Python, as it is easy to implement and understand. But at the same time, it also has some disadvantages in creating visually appealing graphics to the end users.

Here are a couple of other tools you can consider for data visualization in Python.

Chaco

It is best suited for interactive visualization and static plotting. It has excellent features to express complex data visualizations having many inter connections. Its rendering is pretty faster as compared to matplotlib.

You can find more details at this link:
http://code.enthought.com/chaco/

Mayavi

It was created by P. Ramachandran and is basically a 3-Dimensional toolkit. It integrates easily with Python without any issues. We can easily rotate, pan, or zoom the plots with the help of keyboard or mouse.

You can find more details at this link:

https://docs.enthought.com/mayavi/mayavi/

You now have the beginner tools to implement the features of Python. Be patient with yourself and enjoy your journey in the amazing world of Python.

References

- http://pandas.pydata.org

- http://www.codebasicshub.com/

- Source of screenshot: Jupyter Notebook (kernel: Python 3)

- www.google.com